Informing the legislative debate since 1914

Navy Aegis Ballistic Missile Defense (BMD) Program: Background and Issues for Congress

Ronald O'Rourke

Specialist in Naval Affairs

June 20, 2014

Congressional Research Service

7-5700

www.crs.gov

RL33745

Summary

The Aegis ballistic missile defense (BMD) program, which is carried out by the Missile Defense Agency (MDA) and the Navy, gives Navy Aegis cruisers and destroyers a capability for conducting BMD operations. Under MDA and Navy plans, the number of BMD-capable Navy Aegis ships is scheduled to grow from 33 at the end of FY2014 to 43 at the end of FY2019. The figure of 43 ships for FY2019, however, includes four BMD-capable Aegis cruisers that are proposed under the Navy's FY2015 budget for some form of reduced operating status starting in FY2015.

Under the Administration's European Phased Adaptive Approach (EPAA) for European BMD operations, BMD-capable Aegis ships are operating in European waters to defend Europe from potential ballistic missile attacks from countries such as Iran. On October 5, 2011, the United States, Spain, and NATO jointly announced that, as part of the EPAA, four BMD-capable Aegis ships are to be forward-homeported (i.e., based) at Rota, Spain, in FY2014 and FY2015. BMD-capable Aegis ships also operate in the Western Pacific and the Persian Gulf to provide regional defense against potential ballistic missile attacks from countries such as North Korea and Iran.

The Aegis BMD program is funded mostly through MDA's budget. The Navy's budget provides additional funding for BMD-related efforts. MDA's proposed FY2014 budget requests a total of $2,046.3 million in procurement and research and development funding for Aegis BMD efforts, including funding for two Aegis Ashore sites in Poland and Romania that are to be part of the EPAA. MDA's budget also includes operations and maintenance (O&M) and military construction (MilCon) funding for the Aegis BMD program.

Issues for Congress regarding the Aegis BMD program include the following:

- burden-sharing—how European naval contributions to European BMD capabilities and operations compare to U.S. naval contributions to European BMD capabilities and operations;

- the Navy's proposal to place four BMD-capable Aegis cruisers into some form of reduced operational status starting in FY2015;

- a proposed reduction in planned numbers of SM-3 interceptors to be procured;

- the lack of a target for simulating the endo-atmospheric (i.e., final) phase of flight of China's DF-21 anti-ship ballistic missile; and

- concurrency and technical risk in the Aegis BMD program.

Contents

Tables

Appendixes

Contacts

Introduction

This report provides background information and issues for Congress on the Aegis ballistic missile defense (BMD) program, which is carried out by the Missile Defense Agency (MDA) and the Navy, and gives Navy Aegis cruisers and destroyers a capability for conducting BMD operations. Congress's decisions on the Aegis BMD program could significantly affect U.S. BMD capabilities and funding requirements, and the BMD-related industrial base.

Background

Aegis Ships

The Navy's cruisers and destroyers are called Aegis ships because they are equipped with the Aegis ship combat system—an integrated collection of sensors, computers, software, displays, weapon launchers, and weapons named for the mythological shield that defended Zeus. The Aegis system was originally developed in the 1970s for defending ships against aircraft, anti-ship cruise missiles (ASCMs), surface threats, and subsurface threats. The system was first deployed by the Navy in 1983, and it has been updated many times since. The Navy's Aegis ships include Ticonderoga (CG-47) class cruisers and Arleigh Burke (DDG-51) class destroyers.

Ticonderoga (CG-47) Class Aegis Cruisers

Overview

A total of 27 CG-47s (CGs 47 through 73) were procured for the Navy between FY1978 and FY1988; the ships entered service between 1983 and 1994. The first five ships in the class (CGs 47 through 51), which were built to an earlier technical standard in certain respects, were judged by the Navy to be too expensive to modernize and were removed from service in 2004-2005, leaving 22 ships in operation (CGs 52 through 73).

Proposal to Place Four BMD-Capable Aegis Cruisers in Reduced Operating Status

As a cost-saving measure, the Navy's FY2015 budget proposes putting the 11 youngest Aegis cruisers (CGs 63 through 73) into some form of reduced operating status starting in FY2015. While in reduced operating status, the ships would be modernized in preparation for their eventual return to full operational status. The ships would be returned to full operational status years from now, as one-for-one replacements for the 11 older Aegis cruisers that are to remain in full operational status (CGs 52 through 62), as each of those 11 older cruisers reaches the end of its service life.

Among the 11 Aegis cruisers that are proposed for reduced operating status under the Navy's proposed FY2015 budget are four that are BMD-capable—CG-67 (*Shiloh*), CG-70 (*Lake Erie*),

CG-72 (*Vella Gulf*), and CG-73 (*Port Royal*). Under a reported preliminary version of the Navy's plan, these four ships might return to service in 2024, 2026, 2027, and 2027, respectively.[1]

Arleigh Burke (DDG-51) Class Aegis Destroyers[2]

62 Flight I/II and Flight IIA DDG-51s Procured in FY1985-FY2005

A total of 62 DDG-51s were procured for the Navy between FY1985 and FY2005; the first entered service in 1991 and the 62nd entered service in FY2012. The first 28 ships, known as Flight I/II DDG-51s, are scheduled to remain in service until age 35. The next 34 ships, known as Flight IIA DDG-51s, incorporate some design changes and are scheduled to remain in service until age 40.

No DDG-51s Procured in FY2006-FY2009

No DDG-51s were procured in FY2006-FY2009. The Navy during this period instead procured three Zumwalt (DDG-1000) class destroyers. The DDG-1000 design does not use the Aegis system and does not include a capability for conducting BMD operations. Navy plans do not call for modifying DDG-1000s to make them BMD-capable.

11 Flight IIA DDG-51s Procured or Programmed for FY2010-FY2016

Procurement of Flight IIA DDG-51s resumed in FY2010. A total of eight were procured in FY2010-FY2014, in annual quantities of 1, 2, 1, 3, and 1, respectively. Navy plans call for procuring two more Flight IIA DDG-51s in FY2015, and one more Flight IIA DDG-51—the final Flight IIA ship—in FY2016. The ship procured in FY2010 is scheduled to enter service in FY2016.

Flight III DDG-51s Programmed Starting in FY2016

Navy plans call for shifting to procurement of a new version of the DDG-51, called the Flight III version, starting in FY2016. Of the two DDG-51s scheduled for procurement in FY2016, one is to be the final Flight IIA ship, and the other is to be the first Flight III ship. The Flight III version is to be equipped with a new radar, called the Air and Missile Defense Radar (AMDR), that is more capable than the SPY-1 radar installed on all previous Aegis cruisers and destroyers.

Projected Aegis Ship Force Levels

The Navy's FY2015 30-year (FY2015-FY2043) shipbuilding plan projects that the total number of Aegis cruisers and destroyers will be between 80 and 97 during the 30-year period.[3]

---

[1] See USNI News Editor, "Navy's New 'Battle Force' Tally To Include Hospital Ships and Small Patrol Craft," *USNI News* (http://news.usni.org), March 11, 2014.

[2] For more on the DDG-51 program, see CRS Report RL32109, *Navy DDG-51 and DDG-1000 Destroyer Programs: Background and Issues for Congress*, by Ronald O'Rourke.

[3] For a table showing the total number of cruisers and destroyers each year from FY2015 through FY2044, see CRS Report RL32665, *Navy Force Structure and Shipbuilding Plans: Background and Issues for Congress*, by Ronald (continued...)

Aegis Ships in Allied Navies

Sales of the Aegis system to allied countries began in the late 1980s. Allied countries that now operate, are building, or are planning to build Aegis-equipped ships include Japan, South Korea, Australia, Spain, and Norway.[4]

Aegis BMD System[5]

Aegis ships are given a capability for conducting BMD operations by incorporating changes to the Aegis system's computers and software, and by arming the ships with BMD interceptor missiles. In-service Aegis ships can be modified to become BMD-capable ships, and DDG-51s procured in FY2010 and subsequent years are to be built from the start with a BMD capability.

Versions of Aegis BMD System

Currently fielded versions of the Aegis BMD system are called the 3.6.X version and the newer and more capable 4.X version. MDA and Navy plans call for fielding increasingly capable versions in coming years; these planned versions are called 5.0, 5.0 CU (meaning capability upgrade), and 5.1. Improved versions feature improved processors and software, and are to be capable of using improved versions of the SM-3 interceptor missile (see **Table 1** below). BMD-capable Aegis ships can have their BMD capabilities upgraded from earlier versions to later versions.

Aegis BMD Interceptor Missiles

The BMD interceptor missiles used by Aegis ships are the Standard Missile-3 (SM-3) and the Standard Missile-2 Block IV (SM-2 Block IV). The SM-2 Block IV is to be succeeded in coming years by a BMD version of the new SM-6 interceptor.

SM-3 Midcourse Interceptor

The SM-3 is designed to intercept ballistic missiles above the atmosphere (i.e., exo-atmospheric intercept), in the midcourse phase of an enemy ballistic missile's flight. It is equipped with a "hit-to-kill" warhead, called a kinetic warhead, that is designed to destroy a ballistic missile's warhead by colliding with it.

MDA and Navy plans call for fielding increasingly capable versions of the SM-3 in coming years. The current version, called the SM-3 Block IA, is now being supplemented by the more capable SM-3 Block IB. These are to be followed by the even more capable SM-3 Block IIA.

(...continued)

O'Rourke. The totals shown in these two reports include the three Zumwalt (DDG-1000) class destroyers, which are to enter service in FY2014, FY2016, and FY2018; these non-Aegis ships would need to be subtracted out of the figures shown in the tables to get the figures for the total number of Aegis ships.

[4] The Norwegian ships are somewhat smaller than the other Aegis ships, and consequently carry a reduced-size version of the Aegis system that includes a smaller, less-powerful version of the SPY-1 radar.

[5] Unless stated otherwise, information in this section is taken from MDA briefings on the Aegis BMD program given to CRS and CBO analysts in March 2010, March 2011, March 2012, and April 2013.

Compared to the Block IA version, the Block IB version has an improved (two-color) target seeker, an advanced signal processor, and an improved divert/attitude control system for adjusting its course.

In contrast to the Block IA and 1B versions, which have a 21-inch-diameter booster stage at the bottom but are 13.5 inches in diameter along the remainder of their lengths, the Block IIA version has a 21-inch diameter along its entire length. The increase in diameter to a uniform 21 inches provides more room for rocket fuel, permitting the Block IIA version to have a burnout velocity (a maximum velocity, reached at the time the propulsion stack burns out) that is greater than that of the Block IA and IB versions,[6] as well as a larger-diameter kinetic warhead. The United States and Japan have cooperated in developing certain technologies for the Block IIA version, with Japan funding a significant share of the effort.[7]

Until recently, a more capable missile called the SM-3 Block IIB was also planned. Compared to the Block IIA, the Block IIB version was to include a lighter kill vehicle, flexible propulsion, and upgraded fire control software.[8] On March 15, 2013, however, the Department of Defense (DOD) announced that it was

- "restructuring" (i.e., canceling) the SM-3 Block IIB program;

- shifting funding from SM-3 Block IIB program to other BMD efforts (specifically, the Ground Based Interceptor (GBI) BMD program in Alaska and to earlier versions of the SM-3); and

- dropping Phase IV of the European Phased Adaptive Approach (or EPAA—see discussion below), which was to feature the deployment of the SM-3 Block IIB missile.[9]

---

[6] Some press reports and journal articles, all of which are now a decade or more old, report unconfirmed figures on the burnout velocities of various SM-3 missile configurations (some of which were proposed but ultimately not pursued). See, for example, J. D. Marshall, *The Future Of Aegis Ballistic Missile Defense*, point paper dated October 15, 2004, accessed online at http://www.marshall.org/pdf/materials/259.pdf; "STANDARD Missile-3 Destroys a Ballistic Missile Target in Test of Sea-based Missile Defense System," Raytheon news release circa January 26, 2002; Gopal Ratnam, "U.S. Navy To Play Larger Role In Missile Defense, *Defense News*, January 21-27, 2002: 10; Hans Mark, "A White Paper on the Defense Against Ballistic Missiles," *The Bridge*, Summer 2001, pp. 17-26, accessed online at http://www.nae.edu/nae/bridgecom nsf/weblinks/NAEW-63BM86/$FILE/BrSum01.pdf?OpenElement; Michael C. Sirak, "White House Decision May Move Sea-Based NMD Into Spotlight," *Inside Missile Defense*, September 6, 2000: 1; Henry F. Cooper and J.D. Williams, "The Earliest Deployment Option—Sea-Based Defenses," *Inside Missile Defense*, September 6, 2000 (guest perspective; including graphic on page 21); Robert Holzer, "DoD Weighs Navy Interceptor Options, *Defense News*, July 24, 2000: 1, 60 (graphic on page 1); and Robert Holzer, "U.S. Navy Gathers Strength, Allies in NMD Showdown," *Defense News*, March 15, 1999: 1, 42 (graphic on page 1).

[7] The cooperative research effort has been carried out under a U.S.-Japan memorandum of agreement signed in 1999. The effort has focused on risk reduction for four parts of the missile: the sensor, an advanced kinetic warhead, the second-stage propulsion, and a lightweight nose cone. The Block IIA development effort includes the development of a missile, called the Block II, as a stepping stone to the Block IIA. As a result, the Block IIA development effort has sometimes been called the Block II/IIA development effort. The Block II missile is not planned as a fielded capability.

[8] Source: H.Rept. 111-491 of May 21, 2010 (the House Armed Services Committee report on H.R. 5136, the FY2011 defense authorization bill), p. 196.

[9] See Missile Defense Announcement, As Delivered by Secretary of Defense Chuck Hagel, The Pentagon, Friday, March 15, 2013, accessed March 20, 2013, at http://www.defense.gov/speeches/speech.aspx?speechid=1759, and DOD news transcript, "DOD News Briefing on Missile Defense from the Pentagon," March 15, 2013, accessed March 20, 2013, at http://www.defense.gov/transcripts/transcript.aspx?transcriptid=5205.

MDA states that that SM-3 Block IBs have an estimated unit procurement cost of about $10 million to $12 million, and that SM-3 Block IIAs have an estimated unit procurement cost of about $20 million to $24 million.

SM-2 and SM-6 Terminal Interceptors

The SM-2 Block IV is designed to intercept ballistic missiles inside the atmosphere (i.e., endo-atmospheric intercept), during the terminal phase of an enemy ballistic missile's flight. It is equipped with a blast fragmentation warhead. The existing inventory of SM-2 Block IVs—72 as of February 2012—was created by modifying SM-2s that were originally built to intercept aircraft and ASCMs. A total of 75 SM-2 Block IVs were modified, and 3 have been used in BMD flight tests.

MDA and Navy plans call for developing and procuring a more capable terminal-phase BMD interceptor based on the SM-6 air defense missile (the successor to the SM-2 air defense missile). The initial version of the SM-6 BMD interceptor, called Increment 1, is to enter service around 2015; a subsequent version, called Increment 2, is to enter service around 2018.

Summary of Aegis BMD Versions

Table 1 summarizes the various versions of the Aegis BMD system and correlates them with the phases of the European Phased Adaptive Approach (or EPAA; see below) for European BMD operations.

Table 1. Versions of Aegis BMD System

EPAA Phase	Phase I	Phase II		Phase III
Version of Aegis BMD system	**3.6.X**	**4.X**	**5.0/5.0 CU**	**5.1**
Certified for use	2006	2012	2014/2015	2018
OTE assessment	2008	2014	2016	2020
SM-3 missile variants used for exo-atmospheric intercepts				
SM-3 Block IA	X	X	X	X
SM-3 Block IB	X[a]	X	X	X
SM-3 Block IIA				X
SM-2 and SM-6 missile variants used for endo-atmospheric (terminal) intercepts				
SM-2 Block IV	X		X	
SM-6 Increment 1		X	X	X
SM-6 Increment 2				X
Types of ballistic missiles that can be countered				
SRBM	Yes	Yes	Yes	Yes
MRBM	Yes	Yes	Yes	Yes
IRBM	Yes (Limited)	Yes	Yes	Yes (Enhanced)
ICBM	No[b]	No[b]	No[b]	No[b]
Capability for launch on remote or engage on remote				
Launch on remote	Yes (Initial)	Yes (Enhanced)	Yes (Enhanced)	Yes (Enhanced)
Engage on remote	No	No	No	Yes

Source: Table prepared by CRS based on MDA FY2015 budget briefing.

Notes: OTE is operational test and evaluation. **SRBM** is short-range ballistic missile; **MRBM** is medium-range ballistic missile; **IRBM** is intermediate-range ballistic missile; **ICBM** is intercontinental ballistic missile. **Launch on remote** is the ability to launch the interceptor using data from off-board sensors. **Engage on remote** is the ability to engage targets using data from off-board sensors.

a. Capability for using SM-3 Block IB added through capability, maintenance, and inventory update for the 3.6.3 version.

b. Cannot intercept ICBMs, but the system has a long-range search and track (LRS&T) capability—an ability to detect and track ballistic missiles at long ranges. In the FY2014 budget submission, the 5.1 version was described as having "some limited" capability against ICBMs.

European Phased Adaptive Approach (EPAA) for European BMD

On September 17, 2009, the Obama Administration announced a new approach for regional BMD operations called the Phased Adaptive Approach (PAA). The first application of the approach is in Europe, and is called the European PAA (EPAA). EPAA calls for using BMD-capable Aegis ships, a land-based radar in Europe, and eventually two Aegis Ashore sites in Romania and Poland to defend Europe against ballistic missile threats from countries such as Iran. Phase I of EPAA involved deploying Aegis BMD ships and a land-based radar in Europe by the end of 2011. Phase II involves establishing the Aegis Ashore site in Romania with SM-3 IB interceptors in the 2015 timeframe. Phase 3 involves establishing the Aegis Ashore site in Poland with SM-3 IIA interceptors in the 2018 timeframe. Each Aegis Ashore site in the EPAA is to include a structure housing an Aegis system similar to the deckhouse on an Aegis ship and 24 SM-3 missiles launched from a re-locatable Vertical Launch System (VLS) based on the VLS that is installed in

Navy Aegis ships. Although BMD-capable Aegis ships have deployed to European waters before 2011, the first BMD-capable Aegis ship officially deployed to European waters as part of the EPAA departed its home port of Norfolk, VA, on March 7, 2011, for a deployment to the Mediterranean that lasted several months.[10]

Planned Numbers of BMD-Capable Aegis Ships and SM-3 Interceptors

As shown in **Table 2**, under MDA and Navy plans, the number of BMD-capable Navy Aegis ships is scheduled to grow from 33 at the end of FY2014 to 43 at the end of FY2019. As also shown in the table, however, the figure of 43 ships for FY2019 includes the four BMD-capable Aegis cruisers that are proposed under the Navy's FY2015 budget for some form of reduced operating status starting in FY2015 (see "Ticonderoga (CG-47) Class Aegis Cruisers" above).

---

[10] Karen Parrish, "Milestone nears for European Missile Defense Plan," *American Forces Press Service*, March 2, 2011 (accessed online at http://www.defense.gov/news/newsarticle.aspx?id=62997); Untitled "Eye On The Fleet" news item, *Navy News Service*, March 7, 2011 (accessed online at http://www navy mil/view_single.asp?id=98184); "Warship With Radar Going To Mediterranean," *Washington Post*, March 2, 2011; Brock Vergakis, "US Warship Deploys to Mediterranean to Protect Europe Form Ballistic Missiles, *Canadian Press*, March 7, 2011.

Table 2. Numbers of BMD-Capable Aegis Ships and SM-3 Missiles

	Prior	FY13	FY14	FY15 (req.)	FY16 (proj.)	FY17 (proj.)	FY18 proj.)	FY19 (proj.)
BMD-capable Aegis ships								
BMD conversions of existing Aegis cruisers and destroyers (cumulative totals)								
3.6.1 version	24	22	24	21	17	17	17	17
4.0.1 version	3	6	7	9	10	10	10	10
5.0 version	1	2	2	3	6	7	6	3
5.1 version	0	0	0	0	0	0	3	8
Subtotal	28	30	33	33	33	34	36	38
New Aegis destroyers procured in FY2010 and beyond, with BMD installed during construction (cumulative totals)								
5.0 version	0	0	0	0	3	3	4	5
TOTAL	28	30	33	33	36	37	40	43
Aegis cruisers proposed for reduced operating status starting in FY15	0	0	0	4	4	4	4	4
TOTAL excluding Aegis cruisers in above line	28	30	33	29	32	33	36	39
SM-3 missile cumulative procurement / delivery / inventory quantities (including RDT&E purchases)								
Block I/IA	150 / 113 / 93	150 / 113 / 90	150 / 141 / 118	150 / 150 / 118	150 / 150 / 101	150 / 150 / 83	150 / 150 / 58	150 / 150 / 44
Block IB	35 / 3 / 0	68 / 13 / 7	120 / 35 / 26	150 / 60 / 44	198 / 107 / 91	240 / 142 / 126	281 / 186 / 170	332 / 229 / 212
Block IIA	0 / 0 / 0	0 / 0 / 0	0 / 0 / 0	17 / 0 / 0	17 / 0 / 0	27 / 2 / 2	40 / 10 / 6	61 / 17 / 11
Total	185 / 116 / 93	218 / 126 / 97	270 / 176 / 144	317 / 210 / 162	365 / 257 / 192	417 / 294 / 211	471 / 346 / 234	543 / 396 / 267

Source: Table prepared by CRS based on MDA FY2015 budget submission.

October 5, 2011, Announcement of Homeporting in Spain

On October 5, 2011, the United States, Spain, and NATO jointly announced that, as part of the EPAA, four BMD-capable Aegis ships are to be forward-homeported (i.e., based) at the naval base at Rota, Spain.[11] The four ships are the destroyers *Ross* (DDG-71) and *Donald Cook* (DDG-75), which are to move to Rota in FY2014, and the destroyers *Carney* (DDG-64) and *Porter*

---

[11] "Announcement on missile defence cooperation by NATO Secretary General Anders Fogh Rasmussen, the Prime Minister of Spain, Jose Luis Rodriguez Zapatero and US Defense Secretary Leon Panetta," October 5, 2011, accessed October 6, 2011, at http://www.nato.int/cps/en/SID-107ADE55-FF83A6B8/natolive/opinions_78838.htm. See also "SECDEF Announces Stationing of Aegis Ships at Rota, Spain," accessed October 6, 2011, at http://www.navy.mil/search/display.asp?story_id=63109.

(DDG-78), which are to move to Rota in FY2015. As of early 2012, *Carney* was homeported at Mayport, FL, and the other three ships were homeported at Norfolk.[12] The move is to involve an estimated 1,239 military billets (including 1,204 crew members for the four ships and 35 shore-based support personnel),[13] and about 2,100 family members.[14] The Navy estimates the up-front costs of transferring the four ships at $92 million in FY2013, and the recurring costs of basing the four ships in Spain rather than in the United States at roughly $100 million per year.[15]

Rota is on the southwestern Atlantic coast of Spain, a few miles northwest of Cadiz, and about 65 miles northwest of the Strait of Gibraltar leading into the Mediterranean. U.S. Navy ships have been homeported at Rota at various points in the past, most recently in 1979.[16] For additional background information on the Navy's plan to homeport four BMD-capable Aegis destroyers at Rota, Spain, see **Appendix B**.

Aegis BMD Flight Tests

DOD states that since January 2002, the Aegis BMD system has achieved 25 successful exo-atmospheric intercepts in 31 attempts using the SM-3 missile (including 3 successful intercepts in 4 attempts by Japanese Aegis ships), and 3 successful endo-atmospheric intercepts in 3 attempts using the SM-2 Block IV missile, making for a combined total of 28 successful intercepts in 34 attempts.

In addition, on February 20, 2008, a BMD-capable Aegis cruiser operating northwest of Hawaii used a modified version of the Aegis BMD system to shoot down an inoperable U.S. surveillance satellite that was in a deteriorating orbit.[17] Including this intercept in the count increases the totals

---

[12] See "Navy Names Forward Deployed Ships to Rota, Spain," *Navy News Service*, February 16, 2012, accessed online at http://www.navy.mil/search/display.asp?story_id=65393; Kate Wiltrout, "Three Norfolk-Based Navy Ships To Move To Spain," *Norfolk Virginian-Pilot*, February 17, 2012; "Bound for Spain, *Inside the Navy*, February 20, 2012.

[13] Source: Navy information paper dated March 8, 2012, provided by Navy Office of Legislative Affairs to CRS on March 9, 2012.

[14] Source: Navy briefing slides dated February 27, 2012, provided by the Navy to CRS on March 9, 2012.

[15] Source: Navy briefing slides dated February 27, 2012, provided by the Navy to CRS on March 9, 2012. The briefing slides state that the estimated up-front cost of $92 million includes $13.5 million for constructing a new weapon magazine, $0.8 million for constructing a pier laydown area, $3.4 million for constructing a warehouse, $5.0 million for repairing an existing facility that is to be used as an administrative/operations space, and $69.3 million for conducting maintenance work on the four ships in the United States prior to moving them to Rota. The briefing states that the estimated recurring cost of $100 million per year includes costs for base operating support, annual PCS (personnel change of station) costs, a pay and allowances delta, annual mobile training team costs, ship maintenance work, the operation of a Ship Support Activity, and higher fuel costs associated with a higher operating tempo that is maintained by ships that are homeported in foreign countries.

[16] Source: Sam Fellman, "U.S. To Base Anti-Missile Ships in Spain," *Defense News*, October 10, 2011: 76.

[17] The modifications to the ship's Aegis BMD midcourse system reportedly involved primarily making changes to software. DOD stated that the modifications were of a temporary, one-time nature. Three SM-3 missiles reportedly were modified for the operation. The first modified SM-3 fired by the cruiser successfully intercepted the satellite at an altitude of about 133 nautical miles (some sources provide differing altitudes). The other two modified SM-3s (one carried by the cruiser, another carried by an engage-capable Aegis destroyer) were not fired, and the Navy stated it would reverse the modifications to these two missiles. (For additional information, see the MDA discussion available online at http://www.mda.mil/system/aegis_one_time_mission.html, and also Peter Spiegel, "Navy Missile Hits Falling Spy Satellite," *Los Angeles Times*, February 21, 2008; Marc Kaufman and Josh White, "Navy Missile Hits Satellite, Pentagon Says," *Washington Post*, February 21, 2008; Thom Shanker, "Missile Strikes A Spy Satellite Falling From Its Orbit," *New York Times*, February 21, 2008; Bryan Bender, "US Missile Hits Crippled Satellite," *Boston Globe*, February 21, 2008; Zachary M. Peterson, "Navy Hits Wayward Satellite On First Attempt," *NavyTimes.com*, February
(continued...)

---

to 26 successful exo-atmospheric intercepts in 32 attempts using the SM-3 missile, and 29 successful exo- and endo-atmospheric intercepts in 35 attempts using both SM-3 and SM-2 Block IV missiles.

The Aegis BMD development effort, including Aegis BMD flight tests, is often described as following a development philosophy long-held within the Aegis program office of "build a little, test a little, learn a lot," meaning that development is done in manageable steps, then tested and validated before moving on to the next step.[18]

A January 2014 report on various DOD acquisition programs from DOD's Director, Operational Test and Evaluation (DOT&E)—DOT&E's annual report for FY2013—stated, in the section on the Aegis BMD program, that

Assessment

• In FY13, Aegis BMD demonstrated the capability to perform end-to-end engagements against complex separating short-range and separating medium-range ballistic missiles with the Aegis BMD 4.0 system and SM-3 Block IB guided missiles.

• Flight testing in FY13 exercised Aegis BMD 4.0 launch-on-remote and demonstrated the capability of the 4.0 system to fire deployed SM-3 Block IA guided missiles.

• Test data from FY13, in combination with data collected during previous flight testing, suggest that overall Aegis BMD 4.0 Weapon System reliability is adequate for the midcourse defense mission against short- and medium-range ballistic missiles. However, the SM-3 Block IB third stage rocket motor (TSRM) has experienced flight test failures that require further investigation and the identification of the underlying root cause(s).

• Aegis BMD 4.0's participation in FTG-07 verified the system's capability to perform LRS&T against long-range targets. However, the test highlighted the need to further explore and refine TTPs for the transmission and receipt of Aegis BMD track data for use by GMD.

• With the completion of FTM-21 and FTM-22, the IOT&E flight testing phase for Aegis BMD 4.0 and SM-3 Block IB guided missiles is nearly complete. However, the program needs to complete Flight Test Other-18 (FTX-18) and planned HWIL testing of raid engagement capability and Information Assurance testing using accredited models and

---

(...continued)

21, 2008; Dan Nakaso, "Satellite Smasher Back At Pearl," *Honolulu Advertiser*, February 23, 2008; Zachary M. Peterson, "Lake Erie CO Describes Anti-Satellite Shot," *NavyTimes.com*, February 25, 2008; Anne Mulrine, "The Satellite Shootdown: Behind the Scenes," *U.S. News & World Report*, February 25, 2008; Nick Brown, "US Modified Aegis and SM-3 to Carry Out Satellite Interception Shot," *Jane's International Defence Review*, April 2008: 35.)

MDA states that the incremental cost of the shoot-down operation was $112.4 million when all costs are included. MDA states that this cost is to be paid by MDA and the Pacific Command (PACOM), and that if MDA is directed to absorb the entire cost, "some realignment or reprogramming from other MDA [program] Elements may be necessary to lessen significant adverse impact on [the] AEGIS [BMD program's] cost and schedule." (MDA information paper dated March 7, 2008, provided to CRS on June 6, 2008. See also Jason Sherman, "Total Cost for Shoot-Down of Failed NRO Satellite Climbs Higher," *InsideDefense.com*, May 12, 2008.)

[18] See, for example, "Aegis BMD: "Build a Little, Test a Little, Learn a Lot"," USNI blog, March 15, 2010, accessed September 11, 2013, at http://blog.usni.org/2010/03/15/aegis-bmd-build-a-little-test-a-little-learn-a-lot, and "Aegis Ballistic Missile Defense, Aegis Ballistic Missile Defense Overview for the George C. Marshall Institute, RADM Alan B. Hicks, USN, Aegis BMD Program Director, August 3, 2009, slide 16 of 20, entitled "Some of our Philosophies In a Nutshell (1 of 2)," accessed September 11, 2011, at http://www.marshall.org/pdf/materials/743.pdf.

---

simulations in the test runs-for-the-record before an assessment of effectiveness and suitability can be made. Additionally, the program needs to test Aegis-Aegis, Aegis-THAAD, and Aegis-Patriot engagement coordination; only the first of these three types of engagement coordination is planned for live-target testing before the SM-3 Block IB Full-Rate Production decision in 4QFY14.

• The program has addressed and tested corrections for the SM-3 TSRM problems found in FTM-15 and FTM-16 Event 2.

- The program re-designed the TSRM cold gas regulator in response to the FTM-15 anomalous TSRM behavior; the new cold gas regulator has now been flight tested five times without incident.

- To correct the failure exhibited in the FTM-16 Event 2 TSRM energetic event, the program modified the TSRM's inter-pulse delay time; the now greater minimum inter-pulse delay has been exercised without incident in three flight tests and a number of ground-based static firings.

• During FTM-21, the second of two salvo-launched SM-3 Block IB guided missiles suffered a reliability failure of the TSRM during second pulse operations (the first missile had already achieved a successful intercept). The MDA has established a Failure Review Board to determine the root cause of this failure.

• A Failure Review Board concluded that the failure to intercept in FTI-01 was caused by a faulty memory chip in the SM-3 Block IA guided missile's Inertial Measurement Unit (IMU). The specific brand of IMU with this problem is confined to a small fraction of fielded SM-3 Block IA guided missiles, and the program and U.S. Navy are working to mitigate any potential impact from those rounds. The faulty chip is not present in the IMU's design for the SM-3 Block IB guided missile.

• An Aegis BMD 3.6.2e destroyer, using an SM-3 Block IA guided missile, successfully intercepted its medium-range ballistic missile target during FTO-01. A full assessment of FTO-01 test mission data with respect to the effectiveness, suitability, and interoperability of the participating BMDS elements is ongoing.

• Continued post-deployment system-level ground testing with the Aegis BMD 3.6 system has helped to refine TTPs and overall interoperability of that system with the BMDS. However, the test events routinely demonstrated that inter-element coordination and interoperability are still in need of improvement.

Recommendations

• Status of Previous Recommendations.

- The program addressed the remaining part of the recommendation from FY11 to demonstrate that the SM-3 TSRM problem that caused the failure in FTM-16 Event 2 has been corrected when it completed the FTM-19, FTM-20, and FTM-21 flight missions with TSRM inter-pulse delays at the revised minimum value.

- The program addressed the first recommendation from FY12 to conduct further live-target testing of the Aegis BMD 4.0.2 LRS&T capability when it successfully sent track data for use by GMD fire control in FTG-07.

- The program addressed the second FY12 recommendation to engage a medium-range target before the Full-Rate Production decision for the SM-3 Block IB guided missile to support assessment of midcourse capability when it completed the FTM-22 flight mission.

• FY13 Recommendations. The program should:

1. Conduct flight testing of Aegis BMD 4.0's remote authorized engagement capability against a medium-range ballistic missile or intermediate-range ballistic missile target using an SM-3 Block IB guided missile.

2. Conduct operationally realistic testing that exercises Aegis BMD 4.0's improved engagement coordination with THAAD and Patriot.

3. Continue to assess an Aegis BMD 4.0 intercept mission where the ship simultaneously engages an anti-air warfare target to verify BMD/anti-air warfare capability.

4. Use the Failure Review Board process to identify the failure mechanism responsible for the FTM-21 second missile failure and determine if there is an underlying root cause common to both the FTM-16 Event 2 and FTM-21 second missile failures.

5. Deliver sufficient Aegis BMD 4.0 validation data and evidence to support BMDS modeling and simulation verification, validation, and accreditation of the Aegis HWIL and digital models.[19]

An August 27, 2013, press report states:

> As the U.S. Navy tries to stick to its funding plans for Aegis combat system upgrades, and as successful live-fire tests for the latest software improvements to the system mount, the service is considering flying fewer tests to save money.
>
> "They're looking at ways to consolidate life-fire tests to save some bucks," says Jim Sheridan, director of the U.S. Navy's Aegis program for Lockheed Martin, the prime contractor for the combat system and proposed upgrades.
>
> The Navy could shave the number of tests to three from five, Sheridan says, adding that the company supports the measures. "We certainly understand the need," Sheridan says.
>
> Not too long ago, Sheridan had voiced concerns that sequestration and other funding issues would delay shipboard Aegis upgrades and improvements. "With the fielding profile, though," he says, "they are sticking to their guns."
>
> According to Sheridan, reducing the number of tests is more than a fair tradeoff for keeping that upgraded Aegis fielding schedule. However, fewer tests, he says, will create challenges for Lockheed Martin, which has prided itself on an Aegis program that develops a little and tests a lot.
>
> "It will make for more dynamic underways," Sheridan says. "It will be busier on the ships."
>
> A shortened test schedule also will reduce the time between exercises for Lockheed to address any problems it sees during those tests. It will be a challenge, Sheridan says, "to turn around fixes expeditiously."[20]

---

[19] Director, Operational Test and Evaluation, *FY 2013 Annual Report*, January 2014, pp. 305-306.

A September 17, 2013, press report states:

> While the U.S. Navy may be considering truncating some Aegis Combat System missile tests, the nation is still sticking to the planned testing schedule, according to officials for Lockheed Martin, the system's prime contractor.
>
> Navy officials—like everyone else at the Pentagon—have been looking for ways to shave costs to deal with the effects of sequestration and other budgetary concerns. Thanks to the recent round of successful Aegis tests, the service has begun to consider consolidating some Aegis tests to help save money, says Jim Sheridan, director of the U.S. Navy's Aegis program for Lockheed.
>
> For example, the Navy could shave the number of tests to three from five, Sheridan says, adding that the company supports the measures, if they are needed.
>
> But sequestration thus far has had no effect on the Aegis testing schedule, Sheridan said Sept. 10 during a Lockheed update briefing on missile programs.
>
> "There has been no impact," Sheridan says. "Targets are being procured. We are continuing on a path laid out a couple of years ago."
>
> Keith Little, Lockheed spokesman, says, "All planned test events associated with the program of record, as of right now, are fully funded."
>
> But, Little reiterates, the successful Aegis testing thus far gives the Navy options. "Should there be budget challenges in the future, consolidation of some test events might be a cost-saving measure for consideration," he says.[21]

For further discussion of Aegis BMD flight tests—including a May 2010 magazine article and supplementary white paper in which two professors with scientific backgrounds criticize DOD claims of successes in Aegis (and other DOD) BMD flight tests—see **Appendix A**.

Allied Participation and Interest in Aegis BMD Program

Japan

Japan's interest in BMD, and in cooperating with the United States on the issue, was heightened in August 1998 when North Korea test-fired a Taepo Dong-1 ballistic missile that flew over Japan before falling into the Pacific.[22] In addition to cooperating with the United States on development of technologies for the SM-3 Block IIA missile, Japan is modifying all six of its Aegis destroyers with Aegis BMD system, and in November 2013 announced plans to procure two additional

---

(...continued)

[20] Michael Fabey, "U.S. Navy Mulls Cutting Aegis Flight Tests To Save Money," *Aerospace Daily & Defense Report*, August 27, 2013: 1.

[21] Michael Fabey, "Aegis Missile Testing Still On Track, Lockheed Says," *Aerospace Daily & Defense Report*, September 17, 2013: 6.

[22] For a discussion, see CRS Report RL31337, *Japan-U.S. Cooperation on Ballistic Missile Defense: Issues and Prospects*, by Richard P. Cronin. This archived report was last updated on March 19, 2002. See also CRS Report RL33436, *Japan-U.S. Relations: Issues for Congress*, coordinated by Emma Chanlett-Avery.

Aegis destroyers and equip them as well with the Aegis BMD system, which will produce an eventual Japanese force of eight BMD-capable Aegis destroyers. Japanese BMD-capable Aegis ships have conducted four flight tests of the Aegis BMD system using the SM-3 interceptor, achieving three successful exo-atmospheric intercepts.

Other Countries

Other countries that MDA views as potential naval BMD operators (using either the Aegis BMD system or some other system of their own design) include the United Kingdom, the Netherlands, Spain, Germany, Denmark, South Korea, and Australia. As mentioned earlier, Spain, South Korea, and Australia either operate, are building, or are planning to build Aegis ships. The other countries operate destroyers and frigates with different combat systems that may have potential for contributing to BMD operations.

For additional background information on allied participation and interest in the Aegis BMD program, see **Appendix C**.

FY2015 Funding Request

The Aegis BMD program is funded mostly through MDA's budget. The Navy's budget provides additional funding for BMD-related efforts. As shown in **Table 3**, MDA's proposed FY2015 budget requests a total of $2,046.3 million in procurement and research and development funding for Aegis BMD efforts, including funding for the two Aegis Ashore sites that are to be part of the EPAA, which is referred to in the table as funding for the land-based SM-3. MDA's budget also includes operations and maintenance (O&M) and military construction (MilCon) funding for the Aegis BMD program.

Table 3. MDA Funding for Aegis BMD Efforts, FY2014-FY2019

(In millions of dollars, rounded to nearest tenth; totals may not add due to rounding)

	FY14	FY15 (req.)	FY16 (proj.)	FY17 (proj.)	FY18 (proj.)	FY19 (proj.)
Procurement funding						
Aegis BMD Advance Procurement (line 28)	0	68.9	70.2	69.8	88.5	90.2
Aegis BMD (line 30)	580.8	435.4	741.6	976.3	1,091.4	1,293.1
Aegis Ashore Phase III (line 32)	131.4	225.8	36.9	63.7	71.6	0
SUBTOTAL Procurement	**712.2**	**730.1**	**848.7**	**1,109.8**	**1,251.5**	**1,383.3**
RDT&E funding						
Aegis BMD (PE 0603892C) (line 88)	909.9	929.2	955.8	911.1	866.7	721.4
Land-based SM-3 (PE 0604880C) (line 109)	129.4	123.4	32.6	26.3	22.9	17.8
Aegis SM-3 IIA (PE 0604881C) (line 110)	308.5	263.7	175.9	67.5	0	0
SUBTOTAL RDT&E	**1,347.8**	**1,316.3**	**1,164.3**	**1,004.9**	**889.6**	**739.2**
TOTAL	**2,060.0**ᵃ	**2,046.4**	**2,013.0**	**2,114.7**	**2,141.1**	**2,122.5**

Source: Table prepared by CRS based on FY2015 MDA budget-justification books for MDA for Research, Development, Test & Evaluation, Defense-Wide (Volume 2a) and for Procurement, Defense-Wide (Volume 2b).

a. The table includes only line items for which funding is requested in FY2015-FY2019; the total shown for FY2014 consequently excludes funding for line items that received funding in FY2014, but for which no funding is requested for FY2015-FY2019.

Issues for Congress

Burden Sharing: U.S. vs. European Naval Contributions to European BMD

One potential oversight issue for Congress concerns burden sharing—how European naval contributions to European BMD capabilities and operations compare to U.S. naval contributions to European BMD capabilities and operations, particularly in light of constraints on U.S. defense spending, worldwide operational demands for U.S. Navy Aegis ships, and calls by some U.S. and European observers (particularly after Russia's actions in March 2014 to gain control of Crimea) for increased defense efforts by NATO countries in Europe. Potential oversight issues for Congress include the following:

- How does the total value of European naval contributions to European BMD capabilities and operations compare to the total value of the U.S. naval contributions (including the Aegis Ashore sites) to European BMD capabilities and operations?

- Given constraints on U.S. defense spending, worldwide operational demands for U.S. Navy Aegis ships, and calls by some U.S. and European observers for increased defense efforts by NATO countries in Europe—as well as the potential for European countries to purchase or build BMD-capable Aegis ships, upgrade existing ships with BMD capabilities, or purchase Aegis ashore systems—should the United States seek increased investment by European countries in their regional BMD capabilities so as to reduce the need for assigning BMD-capable U.S. Navy Aegis ships to the EPAA? Why should European countries not pay a greater share of the cost of the EPAA, since the primary purpose of the EPAA is to defend Europe against theater-range missiles?

A May 30, 2013, press report states:

> As the missile threats from Iran and North Korea have advanced in recent years, the U.S. has become more invested in Navy cruisers and destroyers that carry the high-tech Aegis radar system and dozens of missile interceptors.
>
> As a result, the ballistic missile defense destroyers and cruisers are a growing capability that is in hot demand from military commanders across the Middle East, Europe and the Pacific....
>
> ... the increasing requirements for the ships also exact another toll on the already strained naval forces. Commanders are routinely forced to extend the ships' deployments, keeping sailors at sea for longer periods and shrinking their time at home.
>
> The USS Stout, which is pierside at the Norfolk Naval Station, returned from its deployment to the Persian Gulf region in June 2011, and its crew is now preparing to go back out this summer. While most Navy cruisers and destroyers deploy for about 6-1/2 months, and then

spend more than three years at home, the missile defense warships are spending up to 7-1/2 months deployed and get a bit more than two years at home between tours.

"They are the most stressed, they have the highest operational tempo of all our forces," [Admiral Bill] Gortney [Commander of U.S. Fleet Forces Command] said. "What we're trying to do in the Navy is to meet that demand at an acceptable personnel tempo for our sailors and their families, as well as allow us to continue to do the maintenance so these ships go to their service life."[23]

Proposal to Place Four BMD-Capable Aegis Cruisers in Reduced Operating Status

Another potential oversight issue for Congress concerns the potential operational implications of the Navy's proposal to place four BMD-capable Aegis cruisers into some form of reduced operational status starting in FY2015 (see "Proposal to Place Four BMD-Capable Aegis Cruisers in Reduced Operating Status" above). As shown in **Table 2**, these four ships represent roughly one-tenth of the Navy's BMD-capable ships in FY2015-FY2019. Potential oversight questions for Congress include the following:

- What impact would the placement of these four ships into some form of reduced operating status have on the operational tempo of the Navy's remaining BMD-capable Aegis ships?

- What impact would the placement of these four ships into some form of reduced operating status have on the Navy's ability to meet its BMD mission demands? How much additional operational risk, if any, would result?

Proposed Reductions in Planned Procurement Quantities of SM-3 Missiles

Another potential oversight issue for Congress concerns a proposed reduction in planned numbers of SM-3 interceptors to be procured. As shown in **Table 4** below, the FY2015 budget submission includes 132 fewer SM-3 interceptors in FY2014-FY2018 than the FY2014 submission, a reduction of about 42%. Potential oversight questions for Congress include the following:

- Is the proposed reduction in planned procurement quantities a result of a revised assessment of operational requirements for SM-3 missiles, or is it simply a result of constraints on planned levels of defense spending?

- What might be the operational impact of the proposed reduction in planned procurement quantities? How much additional operational risk, if any, would result?

- What impact, if any, would the proposed reduction in planned procurement quantities have on SM-3 unit procurement costs?

---

[23] Lolita C. Baldor, "Navy Ships Form First Line Of Missile Defense," *Yahoo.com* (*Associated Press*), May 30, 2013.

Table 4. Planned SM-3 Missile Procurement Quantities

As shown in FY2014 and FY2015 budget submissions

	FY15	FY16	FY17	FY18	FY19
FY14 budget	72	72	84	88	n/a
FY15 budget	30	48	52	54	72
Difference	-42	-24	-32	-34	n/a
Cumulative difference	-42	-66	-98	-132	n/a

Source: Table prepared by CRS based on FY2014 and FY2015 MDA budget-justification books. n/a is not available.

Target for Simulating Endo-Atmospheric Flight of DF-21 ASBM

Another potential oversight issue for Congress concerns the lack of a target for simulating the endo-atmospheric (i.e., final) phase of flight of China's DF-21 anti-ship ballistic missile. DOD's Director, Operational Test and Evaluation (DOT&E), in a December 2011 report (DOT&E's annual report for FY2011), stated:

> **Anti-Ship Ballistic Missile Target**
>
> A threat representative Anti-Ship Ballistic Missile (ASBM) target for operational open-air testing has become an immediate test resource need. China is fielding the DF-21D ASBM, which threatens U.S. and allied surface warships in the Western Pacific. While the Missile Defense Agency has exo-atmospheric targets in development, no program currently exists for an endo-atmospheric target. The endo-atmospheric ASBM target is the Navy's responsibility, but it is not currently budgeted. The Missile Defense Agency estimates the non-recurring expense to develop the exo-atmospheric target was $30 million with each target costing an additional $30 million; the endo-atmospheric target will be more expensive to produce according to missile defense analysts. Numerous Navy acquisition programs will require an ASBM surrogate in the coming years, although a limited number of targets (3-5) may be sufficient to validate analytical models.[24]

A February 28, 2012, press report stated:

> "Numerous programs will require" a test missile to stand in for the Chinese DF-21D, "including self-defense systems used on our carriers and larger amphibious ships to counter anti-ship ballistic missiles," [Michael Gilmore, the Pentagon's director of operational test and evaluation] said in an e-mailed statement....
>
> "No Navy target program exists that adequately represents an anti-ship ballistic missile's trajectory," Gilmore said in the e-mail. The Navy "has not budgeted for any study, development, acquisition or production" of a DF-21D target, he said.
>
> Lieutenant Alana Garas, a Navy spokeswoman, said in an e-mail that the service "acknowledges this is a valid concern and is assessing options to address it. We are unable to provide additional details."...

---

[24] Department of Defense, Director, Operational Test and Evaluation, *FY 2011 Annual Report*, December 2011, p. 294.

Gilmore, the testing chief, said his office first warned the Navy and Pentagon officials in 2008 about the lack of an adequate target. The warnings continued through this year, when the testing office for the first time singled out the DF-21D in its annual public report....

The Navy "can test some, but not necessarily all, potential means of negating anti-ship ballistic missiles," without a test target, Gilmore said.[25]

The December 2012 report from DOT&E (i.e., DOT&E's annual report for FY2012) did not further discuss this issue; a January 21, 2013, press report stated that this is because the details of the issue are classified.[26]

Concurrency and Technical Risk in Aegis BMD Program

Another potential oversight issue for Congress is development-production concurrency and technical risk there is in the Aegis BMD program. Below are comments from Government Accountability Office (GAO) reports and a Missile Defense Executive Board report to Congress and on concurrency and technical risk in certain parts of Aegis BMD program.

Aegis System Modernized Software

An April 2014 GAO report on BMD programs stated the following regarding efforts to develop modernized software for the Aegis system:

[A] Seventeen-month delay in associated development efforts by the Navy increased MDA program cost. To offset this increase, MDA reduced its engineering support which could affect its ability to resolve development challenges if significant issues arise prior to delivery.

Discovery of software defects continues to outpace the program's ability to fix them; fixes may have to be implemented after software is delivered.[27]

SM-3 Block IB Missile

An April 7, 2014, press report stated:

The Pentagon is delaying a full-rate production review of Raytheon's Standard Missile-3 Block IB pending an investigation of a September 2013 intercept failure that could lead to the modification of a component also used in the deployed Block IA variant of the missile.

The review, scheduled for fiscal year 2014, is being pushed off until FY-15, the Defense Department revealed in a March 24 response to a draft Government Accountability Office report, which included the response, on April 1.[28]

---

[25] Tony Capaccio, "Navy Lacks Targets To Test U.S. Defenses Against China Missile," *Bloomberg Government* (*bgov.com*), February 28, 2012.

[26] Christopher J. Castelli, "DOD Testing Chief Drops Public Discussion Of ASBM Target Shortfall," *Inside the Navy*, January 21, 2013.

[27] Government Accountability Office, *Missile Defense[:]Mixed Progress in Achieving Acquisition Goals and Improving Accountability*, GAO-14-351, April 2014, p. 14.

An April 2014 GAO report on BMD programs—the one referred to in the press report above—stated:

> The Aegis BMD SM-3 Block IB program largely overcame previous development challenges and successfully intercepted all targets in its last three flight tests.... These tests are required for a full production decision—the last key production authorization by the Under Secretary of Defense, Acquisition, Technology, and Logistics that would allow MDA to produce the remaining 415 interceptors. However, a missile failure of the second interceptor launched during the September 2013 test could increase production risk if design changes are needed....
>
> As we found in April 2013, the SM-3 Block IB production line has been repeatedly disrupted since 2011 due to flight test anomalies caused by malfunctions in two separate sections of the third-stage rocket motor, and development challenges with the throttleable divert and attitude control system—components that maneuver the interceptor in its later stages of flight. These challenges delayed the SM-3 Block IB full production authorization by more than two years to fiscal year 2015. Largely resolving these previous challenges, in fiscal year 2013 the program received permission to procure 33 additional initial production missiles. Although MDA initially planned to award a contract for 29 SM-3 Block IB missiles in fiscal year 2013, it bought four additional missiles in August 2013 to recover an earlier reduction. That reduction occurred to provide funds to resolve technical and production issues. Based on successful intercepts of the last three flight tests, the program also received permission to buy 52 more interceptors in fiscal year 2014.
>
> Despite the three successful intercepts, the effect of the missile failure in September 2013 on the upcoming full production decision remains unclear. Before the program enters into full production, MDA's acquisition management instruction requires it to demonstrate to the Under Secretary of Defense, Acquisition, Technology, and Logistics that there are no significant risks to production and that the planned production quantities are affordable and fully funded. The permission to enter full production is also based on independent assessments of the weapon's effectiveness and suitability by the DOD's Director, Operational Test and Evaluation and the Navy's Commander Operational Test & Evaluation Force. Although the failure investigation is ongoing, preliminary results indicate that the failure occurred in the third-stage rocket motor, a component common to the SM-3 Block IA, which is nearing the end of its production. Different issues with that same component have contributed to previous SM-3 Block IB schedule delays and production disruptions. While the precise cause of the September 2013 failure is under review, MDA documentation indicates that it could potentially result in design changes to the third-stage rocket motor and changes to manufacturing processes. Additionally, retrofits may be required for SM-3 Block IB and SM-3 Block IA interceptors that were already produced. If design changes are necessary, program documentation indicates that they will not be flight tested until the fourth quarter of fiscal year 2015, just prior to the planned deployment of the SM-3 Block IB to support the regional defense of Europe and 6 months after its planned full production decision. Consequently, until the program thoroughly understands the extent of needed modifications, if any, and their effects on performance as demonstrated though testing, its production strategy is at risk of cost growth and schedule delays. MDA has experienced these consequences in other elements when it pursued design changes concurrently with production.[29]

(...continued)

[28] Jason Sherman, "DOD Delays Full-Rate Production Review For SM-3 Block IB," *Inside the Navy*, April 7, 2014.

[29] Government Accountability Office, *Missile Defense[:]Mixed Progress in Achieving Acquisition Goals and Improving Accountability*, GAO-14-351, April 2014, pp. 17-19.

The GAO report recommended that

> To the extent that MDA determines hardware or software modifications are required to address the September 2013 Aegis BMD SM-3 Block IB failure, we recommend that the Secretary of Defense direct,
>
> a) the Director of the MDA to verify the changes work as intended through subsequent flight testing, and
>
> b) the Under Secretary of Defense, Acquisitions, Technology, and Logistics to delay the decision to approve the program's full production until such testing demonstrates that the redesigned missile is effective and suitable.[30]

The GAO report stated that DOD

> partially concurred with our first recommendation to flight test any modifications that may be required to the Aegis BMD SM-3 Block IB as a result of September 2013 failure, before the Under Secretary of Defense, Acquisitions, Technology, and Logistics approves full production. In its comments, DOD acknowledged that if modifications are required they will be tested, but added that the type of testing—flight or ground testing—will depend on the magnitude of such modifications. The department also believes that the component currently tied to the failure, has a successful testing history and thus expects to meet the reliability requirement needed for the full production decision in fiscal year 2015. However, there have now been three flight test anomalies associated with this component over the last three years. According to Aegis BMD officials, they are considering design changes for this component. Since the fiscal year 2015 full production decision is the commitment by the Under Secretary of Defense, Acquisitions, Technology, and Logistics to produce several hundred missiles, this decision should be supported by an assessment of the final product under operational mission conditions to ensure that it is effective and suitable. As such, we maintain our recommendation that before the program is approved for full production, flight testing should demonstrate that any modifications work as intended.[31]

A July 2013 report to Congress by the Missile Defense Executive Board stated the following regarding concurrency in the SM-2 Block IB missile:

> MDA received an early decision from the Under Secretary of Defense for Acquisition, Technology, and Logistics (USD(AT&L)) for initial production of 14 Standard Missile (SM)-3 Block IB missiles. This procurement will provide for timely availability of missiles to support the EPAA Phase 2 Warfighter requirement. This procurement will also sustain suppliers, maintain qualified production lines and maintain SM-3 Block IB missile unit costs. Risk of concurrency is mitigated by the positive results of several SM-3 Block IB flight tests that informed the initial production decision. Subsequently, USD(AT&L) provided an early production decision to procure long lead material for the next lot of 29 SM-3 Block IB missiles and missile canisters. This decision will further enable production missiles to be delivered on a schedule to meet inventory requirements for EPAA Phase 2. The next planned production decisions to approve SM-3 Block IB "all-up-rounds" will also be informed by additional BMDS tests, an initial operational test and evaluation in accordance with title 10, U.S.C., and Knowledge Points (KPs)....

---

[30] Government Accountability Office, *Missile Defense[:]Mixed Progress in Achieving Acquisition Goals and Improving Accountability*, GAO-14-351, April 2014, pp. 27-28.

[31] Government Accountability Office, *Missile Defense[:]Mixed Progress in Achieving Acquisition Goals and Improving Accountability*, GAO-14-351, April 2014, pp. 28-29.

The SM-3 Block IB program office also uses a series of BMDS KPs to identify information to make key decisions about acquisition life-cycle phase transition, funding, technology selections, capability demonstrations, program continuation, selecting an alternative course of action, and managing program risk. MDA KPs are critical to managing development risk at an acceptable level and informing decisions to incorporate technological advances sought by the Warfighter to counter the rapidly advancing threat. This knowledge-based approach measures progress and guides development and production to support an acceptable balance between schedule and risk. Using knowledge-based acquisition decisions in addition to a manageable balance of parallel development and production directly supports BMDS EPAA Phase 2 Warfighter requirements.

In June 2010, through the MDA acquisition oversight process, the alread ongoing SM-3 Block IB (with Aegis Ballistic Missile Defense version 4.0.1) was established in the product development phrase and initial acquisition baselines were set. Development concurrency was mitigated early in the program by leveraging the capability in the SM-3 Block IA missile before acquiring any SM-3 Block IB missiles. SM-3 Block IB missiles use many of the same components as the SM-3 Block IA, including the entire booster stack. The SM-3 Block IB offers more capability against a greater threat set because of improvements in the kinetic warhead (KW). These improvements include a two-color seeker, all reflective optics, an advanced signal processor, and a throttleable control system.

To support SM-3 Block IB development, ground tests were conducted to reduce risk and validate test conditions that are often difficult to duplicate in flight tests. The ground tests mitigated development risk before starting SM-3 Block IB flight tests in 3rd Quarter FY 2011. As a result of problems discovered during flight tests FTM-15 and FTM-16 E2, MDA received congressional approval to convert procurement appropriation funding to research, development, test, and evaluation (RDT&E) funding to resolve those problems before resuming flight tests. Analysis of the flight test results drove additional development to one legacy component as well as an update to the Aegis Weapon System (AWS) version 4.0.2 before the SM-3 Block IB began production. The program office is currently taking delivery of RDT&E missile placed on contract during FY2011. Based on the long lead-time for production, some material had to be procured before flight testing. These RDT&E missiles are supporting final development and testing of the SM-3 Block IB missile.

By direction of the Office of Management and Budget, in 3rd Quarter FY 2012 the program office received a decision from USD(AT&L) to start initial production with the authorization to acquire the first 14 SM-3 Block IB missiles using procurement appropriations. This decision was based on positive results from several SM-3 Block IB flight tests (FTM-16E2a and initial results from FTM-18). This overlap between final aspects of product development and initial production is necessary to sustain suppliers and maintain bioth qualified production lines and SM-3 Block IB missile unit costs.

In addition to the successful flight tests FTM-16E2a and FTM-18 already flown, a number of ground tests and final verification and qualification tests on critical SM-3 Block IB components were conducted prior to the USD(AT&L) decision to authorize long lead material procurement for the next 29 missiles. These steps mitigated potential concurrency between final product development and early material procurement necessary for the next lot of production SM-3 Block IB missiles. Additionally, potential concurrency and concurrency mitigation were reviewed by the MDA Director at the SM-3 Block IB Developmental Baseline Review in 2nd Quarter FY 2013 and progress towards mitigating concurrency is reviewed quarterly by the MDA Director during the SM-3 Block IB BER [Baseline Execution Review]. Finally, the SM-3 Block IB program office plans to participate in a number of additional flight tests tests [sic] including an initial operational test and evaluation in accordance with title 10, U.S.C. (i.e.;, FTM-19, FTM-21, and FTM-22) and complete BMDS KPs to inform the USD(AT&L) decision to approve production of SM-3 Block IB missiles through FY 2017. These sequential production decisions, informed by tailored component qualification tests, other ground tests, and flight tests, minimize concurrency, validate progression from one acquisition phase to the next, and will maintain the schedule necessary to satisfy BMDS EPAA Phase 2 Warfighter requirements.[32]

An April 2013 GAO report stated the following regarding the SM-3 Block IB missile:

> In 2012, the Aegis BMD SM-3 Block IB was able to partially overcome the production and testing issues exacerbated by its concurrent development and production strategy. MDA prematurely began purchasing SM-3 Block IB missiles beyond the number needed for developmental testing in 2010. In 2011, developmental issues arose when the program experienced a failure in its first developmental flight test and an anomaly in a separate SM-3 Block IA flight test, in a component common with the SM-3 Block IB. As a result, production was disrupted when MDA slowed production of the SM-3 Block IB interceptors and reduced planned quantities from 46 to 14. In 2012, the program was able to successfully conduct two flight tests which allowed the program to address some of the production issues by demonstrating a fix made to address one of the 2011 flight test issues. However, development issues continue to delay the program's fiscal year 2012 schedule and production. For example, MDA experienced further difficulties completing testing of a new maneuvering component—contributing to delays for a third flight test needed to validate the SM-3 Block IB capability and also subsequently delaying a production decision for certain components from December 2012 to February 2013.
>
> In order to avoid further disruptions to the production line, the program plans to award the next production contract for some missile components needed for the next order of 29 SM-3 Block IB missiles in February 2013—before the third flight test can verify the most recent software modifications. The program then plans to award the contract to complete this order upon conducting a successful flight test planned for the third quarter of fiscal year 2013.The program is at risk for costly retrofits, additional delays and further production disruptions if issues are discovered during this flight test.[33]

The April 2013 GAO report includes an appendix with additional in-depth discussion of concurrency and technical risk in the SM-3 Block IB program.[34]

SM-3 Block IIA Missile

A July 2013 report to Congress by the Missile Defense Executive Board stated the following regarding concurrency in the SM-2 Block IIA missile:

> In 2010, MDA began an acquisition oversight process to establish SM-3 Block IIA and ABMD [Aegis BMD] 5.1 in the technology development phase and set initial technology acquisition baselines.

---

[32] *Missile Defense Executive Board Report to Congress on Concurrency in Development of Ballistic Missile Defense System Capability*, July 2013, pp. 3 and 7-9. Posted online at InsideDefense.com (subscription required), September 27, 2013. The report was directed by page 82 of the House Armed Services Committee's report (H.Rept. 112-479 of May 11, 2012) on H.R. 4310, the FY2013 National Defense Authorization Act.

[33] Government Accountability Office, *Missile Defense[:] Opportunity to Refocus on Strengthening Acquisition Management*, GAO-13-432, April 2013, pp. 22-23.

[34] Government Accountability Office, *Missile Defense[:] Opportunity to Refocus on Strengthening Acquisition Management*, GAO-13-432, April 2013, Appendix II on pp. 52-59.

The program office will complete development and initial testing of the SM-3 Block IIA using a structured systems engineering approach that aligns with MDA acquisition policy and processes. In February 2010, the SCD [SM-3 Block IIA Cooperative Development] Executive Steering Committee approved the SCD KP [Knowledge Point] plan. The 33 identified KPs define the critical knowledge required during development to ensure successful design and initial testing. The structured systems engineering and knowledge-based approach eliminates development concurrency for required capability delivery within planned cost and schedule. Additionally, the program office's progress towards mitigating concurrency is reviewed quarterly by the MDA Director during the SM-3 Block IIA BER [Baseline Execution Review].

The program office has begun a robust development and test process using hardware; major test events and KPs precede major acquisition milestones. For example, the program office successfully demonstrated subsystem functional performance and completed subsystem preliminary design reviews (PDRs) for all critical SM-3 Block IIA subsystems (e.g., third stage rocket motor (TSRM), second stage rocket motor (SSRM), booster, nosecone, divert attitude control system (DACS), and the KW [kinetic warhead]) well in advance of the March 2012 system PDR. The subsystem reviews used data from computer in the loop (CIL) tests and data fro[m] hardware testing from two full-duration DACS valve hot-fire tests, three Japanese rocket motor firings, and Japanese nosecone separation testing.

SM-3 Block IIA will continue this rigorous engineering review process focused on hardware performance to prepare and inform the move from the technology development phase to product development. The SCD critical design review (CDR) of the interface with the Aegis BMD 5.1 weapon system for organic operation will be complete before the full SM-3 Block IIA production development decision in the 2nd Quarter FY 2014. The SCD CDR will use data from both hardware in the loop (HIL) and CIL tests, and data from hardware tests like a restrained firing of the MK-72 booster, a propulsion test vehicle test, and hot-fire test events on the DACS, SSRN, and TSRM. The full system CRS (planned for 1st Quarter FY 2015) will incorporate results from the missile system CDRs, VLS CDRs, canister CDR, KPs, and testing, using organic ABMD 5.1 weapon and missile system interface.

The rigorous engineering process will continue to inform decisions as SM-3 Block IIA moves from product development to the production phase. Performance data from HIL and CIL tests will be augmented with flight test data to support knowledge-based decisions. Initial flight tests will focus on validating propulsion system performance in flight using CTVs [control test vehicles]. Subsequent flight tests will demonstrate missile functionality and intercept capability, and prior to a full production decision, will culminate in an initial operational test and evaluation in accordance with title 10, U.S.C. Flight tests will be spaced from 1 year to 6 months so that lessons learned are incorporated into the design before the next test.[35]

An April 2013 GAO report stated the following regarding the SM-3 Block IIA missile:

MDA has taken steps to reduce acquisition risk by decreasing the overlap between technology development and product development for two of its programs—the Aegis BMD SM-3 Block IIA and the [now-terminated] SM-3 Block IIB programs. Reconciling gaps between requirements and available resources before product development begins makes it more likely that a program will meet cost, schedule, and performance targets.

---

[35] *Missile Defense Executive Board Report to Congress on Concurrency in Development of Ballistic Missile Defense System Capability*, July 2013, pp. 9-10. Posted online at InsideDefense.com (subscription required), September 27, 2013. The report was directed by page 82 of the House Armed Services Committee's report (H.Rept. 112-479 of May 11, 2012) on H.R. 4310, the FY2013 National Defense Authorization Act.

- The Aegis BMD SM-3 Block IIA program added time and money to the program to extend development. Following significant technology development problems with four components, MDA delayed the system preliminary design review—during which a program demonstrates that the technologies and resources available are aligned with requirements—for more than 1 year, thereby reducing its acquisition risk. As a result, in March 2012, following additional development of the four components, the program was able to successfully complete the review.[36]

The April 2013 GAO report includes an appendix with additional in-depth discussion of concurrency and technical risk in the SM-3 Block IIA program.[37]

Aegis Ashore

An April 2014 GAO report on BMD programs states the following regarding the Aegis Ashore development effort:

> MDA plans to complete development of the first operational facility and award a contract to begin the second before flight testing demonstrates that the facility works with the Aegis modernized weapon system software and interceptors as intended.
>
> Flight test delays and cancellations, as well as challenges with development of the Aegis modernized weapon system software increase the risk of discovering performance issues that may require fixes after operational deployment.[38]

A July 2013 report to Congress by the Missile Defense Executive Board stated the following regarding concurrency in the SM-2 Block IB missile:

> The Aegis Ashore element is leveraging and reusing the development and design from several United States Navy programs with similar components. For example, the Aegis Ashore vertical launch system (VLS) is the same system previously procured for the cruiser and destroyer programs. The deckhouse design is similar to the destroyer configuration for the Aegis SPY radar arrays. The Aegis Ashore program office will also use a number of BMDS KPs [Knowledge Points] and flight tests, including an operational test at the Pacific Missile Range Facility, from other MDA elements to mitigate risk and inform major program decisions....
>
> In June 2010, through the MDA acquisition oversight process, Aegis Ashore was established in the product development phase and initial acquisition baselines were set. The current Aegis Ashore acquisition strategy has balanced development concurrency with flight tests, military construction and component procurement decisions. It has an appropriately aligned strategy with the necessary levels of testing, monitored by knowledge-based decision points. Aegis Ashore uses ongoing development from United State navy ASW [Aegis Weapon System] program. The AWS supporting Aegis Ashore is the same system supporting all Aegis shipbuilding programs (past and present). Before the first Aegis Ashore flight test, the SM-3 Block IB missile will have been tested several times with the AWS.

---

[36] Government Accountability Office, *Missile Defense[:] Opportunity to Refocus on Strengthening Acquisition Management*, GAO-13-432, April 2013, p. 21.

[37] Government Accountability Office, *Missile Defense[:] Opportunity to Refocus on Strengthening Acquisition Management*, GAO-13-432, April 2013, Appendix IV on pp. 70-72.

[38] Government Accountability Office, *Missile Defense[:]Mixed Progress in Achieving Acquisition Goals and Improving Accountability*, GAO-14-351, April 2014, p. 14.

Significant activities during the Aegis Ashore product development phase include integrating the MK41 VLS launcher. The VLS housing is a stell modular structure because there is no ship structure to surround the launcher. This structure design is new, but replicates what was field-tested with other variant of the [S]tandard [M]issile at the White Sands Missile Range, New Mexico. The program office does not expect Aegis Ashore flight-testing to affect the technical design of the MK 41 VLS or the VLS housing.

The deckhouse contains the AWS and hosts the operators who execute the Aegis Ashore mission. This structure is new, not based on an existing design, yet replicates the height and spacing of the Aegis SPY radar arrays similar to a destroyer configuration. Flight-testing is not expected to affect the technical design of the deckhouse.

Aegis Ashore testing includes both weapon system testing to verify performance as the deckhouse is built up, and flight tests to verify communication and controlled fly out of the SM-3 from the MK 41 LVS launcher and will conclude with an operational test at the Pacific Missile Range Facility. This test approach is the same process used in Navy ship construction shake-down trials and combat systems qualifications.

Planning continues for the production of the next and final Aegis Ashore system (based on current requirements and funding). This last system will support EPAA Phase 3. MDA notified USD(AT&L) of their intent to use procurement appropriation funding for Navy program offices to acquire material for this system. The Aegis Ashore program office expects to procure long lead material in 1st Quarter FY 2014. Although the previous Aegis Ashore system will not be completely developed and constructed before the final system begins construction, the last Aegis Ashore system is also based on existing Navy programs and incorporate[s] updates from the previous developmental system. Ground and flight tests from the previous developmental system and other SM-3 flight tests are not expected to impact the design of the final Aegis Ashore system. Progress in maintaining mitigation of potential concurrency risks is reviewed quarterly by the MDA Director during the Aegis Ashore BER [Baseline Execution Review].[39]

An April 2013 GAO report stated the following regarding the Aegis Ashore program:

> The Aegis Ashore program, as we reported in April 2012, initiated product development and established cost, schedule, and performance baselines prior to completing the preliminary design review. Further, we reported that this sequencing increased technical risks and the possibility of cost growth by committing to product development with less technical knowledge than recommended by acquisition best practices and without ensuring that requirements were defined, feasible, and achievable within cost and schedule constraints. In addition, the program committed to buy components necessary for manufacturing prior to conducting flight tests to confirm the system worked as intended. As a result, any design modifications identified through testing would need to be retrofitted to produced items at additional cost. However, the MDA Director stated in March 2012 that the Aegis Ashore development is low risk because of its similarity to the sea-based Aegis BMD.[41] Nonetheless, this concurrent acquisition plan means that knowledge gained from flight tests cannot be used to guide the construction of Aegis Ashore installations or the procurement of components for operational use.[40]

---

[39] *Missile Defense Executive Board Report to Congress on Concurrency in Development of Ballistic Missile Defense System Capability*, July 2013, pp. 3 and 10-11. Posted online at InsideDefense.com (subscription required), September 27, 2013. The report was directed by page 82 of the House Armed Services Committee's report (H.Rept. 112-479 of May 11, 2012) on H.R. 4310, the FY2013 National Defense Authorization Act.

[40] Government Accountability Office, *Missile Defense[:] Opportunity to Refocus on Strengthening Acquisition* (continued...)

The April 2013 GAO report also stated:

> As we reported in April 2012, the instability of content in the Aegis Ashore program's resource baseline obscures our assessment of the program's progress. MDA prematurely set the baseline before program requirements were understood and before the acquisition strategy was firm. The program established its baseline for product development for the Romania and Hawaii facilities in June 2010 with a total cost estimate of $813 million. However 3 days later, when the program submitted this baseline to Congress in the 2010 BAR [BMDS (ballistic missile defense system) Accountability Report], it increased the total cost estimate by 19 percent, to $966 million. Since that time, the program has added a significant amount of content to the resource baseline to respond to acquisition strategy changes and requirements that were added after the baseline was set. Because of these adjustments, from the time the total estimated cost for Aegis Ashore in Romania and Hawaii was first approved in June 2010 at $813 million, it has nearly doubled to its estimate of $1.6 billion reported in the February 2012 BAR. These major adjustments in program content made it impossible to understand annual or longer-term program progress.
>
> These adjustments also affected the schedule baseline for Aegis Ashore. For example, many new activities were added to the baseline in 2012. In addition, comparing the estimated dates for scheduled activities listed in the 2012 BAR to the dates baselined in the 2010 BAR is impossible in some cases because activities from the 2010 BAR were split into multiple events, renamed, or eliminated all together in the 2012 BAR. MDA also redistributed planned activities from the Aegis Ashore schedule baselines into several other Aegis BMD schedule baselines. For example, activities related to software for Aegis Ashore were moved from the Aegis Ashore baseline and were split up and added to two other baselines for the second generation and modernized Aegis weapon systems software. Rearranging content made tracking the progress of these activities against the prior year and original baseline very difficult and in some cases impossible. As a result, appendix III contains a limited schedule assessment of near-term and long-term progress based on activities we were able to track in the BAR. [41]

The April 2013 GAO report also stated:

> Developing and deploying new missile defense systems in Europe to aid in defense of Europe and the United States is a highly complex effort. We reported last year that several of the individual systems that comprise the current U.S. approach to missile defense in Europe—called the European Phased Adaptive Approach—have schedules that are highly concurrent. Concurrency entails proceeding into product development before technologies are mature or into production before a significant amount of independent testing has confirmed that the product works as intended. Such schedules can lead to premature purchases of systems that impair operational readiness and may result in problems that require extensive retrofits, redesigns, and cost increases. A key challenge, therefore, facing DOD is managing individual system acquisitions to keep them synchronized with the planned time frames of the overall U.S. missile defense capability planned in Europe. MDA still needs to deliver some of the capability planned for the first phase of the U.S. missile defense in Europe and is grappling with delays to some systems and/or capabilities planned in each of the next three major deployments. MDA also is challenged by the need to develop the tools, the models and simulations, to understand the capabilities and limitations of the

---

(...continued)

Management, GAO-13-432, April 2013, pp. 24-25.

[41] Government Accountability Office, *Missile Defense[:] Opportunity to Refocus on Strengthening Acquisition Management*, GAO-13-432, April 2013, pp. 33-34.

individual systems before they are deployed. Because of technical limitations in the current approach to modeling missile defense performance, MDA recently chose to undertake a major new effort that it expects will overcome these limitations. However, MDA and the warfighters will not benefit from this new approach until at least half of the four planned phases have deployed....

As we reported in December 2010, the U.S. missile defense approach in Europe commits MDA to delivering systems and associated capabilities on a schedule that requires concurrency among technology, design, testing, and other development activities. We reported in April 2012 that deployment dates were a key factor in the elevated levels of schedule concurrency for several programs. We also reported at that time that concurrent acquisition strategies can affect the operational readiness of our forces and risk delays and cost increases.

DOD declared Phase 1 operational in December 2011, but the systems delivered do not yet provide the full capability planned for the phase. MDA deployed, and the warfighter accepted, Phase 1 with the delivery of an AN/TPY-2 radar, an Aegis BMD ship with SM-3 Block IA missiles, an upgrade to C2BMC, and the existing space-based sensors. Given the limited time between the September 2009 announcement of the U.S. missile defense in Europe and the planned deployment of the first phase in 2011, that first phase was largely defined by existing systems that could be quickly deployed. MDA planned to deploy the first phase in two stages—the systems described above by December 2011 and upgrades to those systems in 2014. Although the agency originally planned to deliver the remaining capabilities of the first phase in 2014, an MDA official told us that MDA now considers these capabilities to be part of the second phase and these capabilities may not be available until 2015.

In addition, independent organizations determined that some of the capabilities that were delivered did not work as intended. For example, the Director, Operational Test and Evaluation reported that there were some interoperability and command and control deficiencies. This organization also reported that MDA is currently investigating these deficiencies.

According to MDA documentation, systems and associated capabilities for the next phases are facing delays, either in development or in integration and testing.

• For Phase 2, some capabilities, such as an Aegis weapon system software upgrade, may not be available. MDA officials stated they are working to resolve this issue.

• For Phase 3, some battle management and Aegis capabilities are currently projected to be delayed and the initial launch of a planned satellite sensor system—PTSS—is delayed.

• For [the now-terminated] Phase 4, deployment of the SM-3 Block IIB missile [was] delayed from 2020 to 2022, and full operational capability of PTSS [was] delayed to no sooner than 2023.[42]

The April 2013 GAO report includes an appendix with additional in-depth discussion of concurrency and technical risk in the Aegis Ashore program.[43]

---

[42] Government Accountability Office, *Missile Defense[:] Opportunity to Refocus on Strengthening Acquisition Management*, GAO-13-432, April 2013, pp. 35 and 37-38.

[43] Government Accountability Office, *Missile Defense[:] Opportunity to Refocus on Strengthening Acquisition Management*, GAO-13-432, April 2013, Appendix III on pp. 60-69.

Legislative Activity for FY2015

Summary of Action on FY2015 MDA Funding Request

Table 5 summarizes congressional action on the FY2015 request for MDA procurement and research and development funding for the Aegis BMD program.

Table 5. Summary of Congressional Action on FY2015 Request for MDA Procurement and RDT&E Funding for Aegis BMD Program

(In millions of dollars, rounded to nearest tenth; totals may not add due to rounding)

	Request	Authorization			Appropriation		
		HASC	SASC	Final	HAC	SAC	Final
Procurement							
Aegis BMD Advance Procurement (line 28)	68.9	68.9	68.9				
Aegis BMD (line 30)	435.4	435.4a	435.4				
Aegis Ashore Phase III (line 32)	225.8	225.8	225.8				
Subtotal Procurement	730.1	730.1a	730.1				
Research, development, test and evaluation (RDT&E)							
Aegis BMD (PE 0603892C) (line 88)	929.2	929.2	929.2				
Land-based SM-3 (PE0604880C) (line 109)	123.4	123.4	123.4				
Aegis SM-3 IIA (PE0604881C) (line 110)	263.7	263.7	263.7				
Subtotal RDT&E	1,316.3	1,316.3	1,316.3				
TOTAL	2,046.4	2,046.4a	2,046.4				

Source: Table prepared by CRS. **For request:** FY2015 budget-justification books for MDA for Research, Development, Test & Evaluation, Defense-Wide (Volume 2a) and for Procurement, Defense-Wide (Volume 2b). **For HASC:** H.Rept. 113-446 of May 13, 2014. **For SASC:** S.Rept. 113-176.

Notes: HASC is House Armed Services Committee; SASC is Senate Armed Services Committee; HAC is House Appropriations Committee; SAC is Senate Appropriations Committee; Conf. is conference.

a.   The amount for Aegis BMD (line 30), and consequently the subtotal for procurement and the total shown at bottom, were subsequently increased by $99 million by House passage of H.Amdt. 688 to H.R. 4435. For details, see "House (Floor Action)"below.

FY2015 National Defense Authorization Act (H.R. 4435/S. 2410)

House (Committee Report)

The House Armed Services Committee, in its report (H.Rept. 113-446 of May 13, 2014) on H.R. 4435, makes the funding recommendations shown in **Table 5**.

Section 1235 of H.R. 4435 as reported states:

SEC. 1235. MISSILE DEFENSE COOPERATION.

(a) Sense of Congress- It is the sense of Congress that—

(1) Admiral Samuel Locklear, Commander of the United States Pacific Command, testified before the Committee on Armed Services of the House of Representatives on March 5, 2014, that in the spring of 2013, North Korea `conducted another underground nuclear test, threatened the use of a nuclear weapon against the United States, and concurrently conducted a mobile missile deployment of an Intermediate Range Ballistic Missile, reportedly capable of ranging our western most U.S. territory in the Pacific.';

(2) General Curtis Scaparrotti, Commander of the United States Forces Korea, testified before such committee on April 2, 2014, that `CFC [Combined Forces Command] is placing special emphasis on missile defense, not only in terms of systems and capabilities, but also with regard to implementing an Alliance counter-missile strategy required for our combined defense.'; and

(3) increased emphasis and cooperation on missile defense among the United States, Japan, and the Republic of Korea, enhances the security of allies of the United States in Northeast Asia, increases the defense of forward-based forces of the United States, and enhances the protection of the United States.

(b) Assessment Required- The Secretary of Defense shall conduct an assessment to identify opportunities for increasing missile defense cooperation among the United States, Japan, and the Republic of Korea, and to evaluate options for short-range missile, rocket, and artillery defense capabilities.

(c) Elements- The assessment under subsection (b) shall include the following:

(1) Candidate areas for increasing missile defense cooperation, including greater information sharing, systems integration, and joint operations.

(2) Potential challenges and limitations to enabling such cooperation and plans for mitigating such challenges and limitations.

(3) An assessment of the utility of short-range missile defense and counter-rocket, artillery, and mortar system capabilities, including with respect to—

(A) the requirements for such capabilities to meet operational and contingency plan requirements in Northeast Asia;

(B) cost, schedule, and availability;

(C) technology maturity and risk; and

(D) consideration of alternatives.

(d) Briefing Required- Not later than 180 days after the date of the enactment of this Act, the Secretary of Defense shall provide to the congressional defense committees a briefing on the assessment under subsection (b).

H.Rept. 113-446 states:

Missile Defense Cooperation With Japan

The committee continues to support the significant level of missile defense cooperation with the Government of Japan. Included in this cooperation is the co-development of the Standard Missile 3 block IIA missile interceptor. Japan is one of only a handful of countries with the requisite technical expertise and with whom the United States has the level of trust required to partner on the development of significant military technology such as a missile interceptor.

The committee is also profoundly appreciative of the continuing activity to deploy a second Army Navy/Transportable Radar Surveillance-model 2 radar unit in Japan. When the radar is available later this year, it will make a significant difference to regional missile defense and the homeland missile defense of the United States. The committee is aware that these two deployments bind together the security of the United States and Japan, and do not come without additional risks to Japanese security. The committee believes this is a measure of the security alliance between the two nations.

The committee commends the announcement of the Secretary of Defense on April 6, 2014, to forward deploy to Japan an additional two United States Navy Aegis Ballistic Missile Defense ships by 2017. The committee supports this decision, as well as Japan's decision to obtain two more Aegis ballistic missile defense ships for its own defense forces.

The committee believes this cooperation is the bedrock of regional security and will support additional missile defense cooperation in the years ahead. (Pages 239-240)

The report also states:

Report on Updated Independent Cost Estimate of the European Phased Adaptive Approach

The committee is aware that the Department of Defense provided the October 2012 Cost Assessment and Program Evaluation (CAPE) Independent Cost Estimate (ICE) for the European Phased Adaptive Approach (EPAA) on February 25, 2014. The committee is aware of both the total acquisition and lifecycle cost as well as the statement of the Under Secretary of Acquisition, Technology and Logistics that there have been numerous requirement content changes to the EPAA since it was completed, including mission requirements.

Therefore, the committee directs the Director, Cost Assessment and Program Evaluation to update his October 2012 ICE and submit it directly to the congressional defense committees not later than November 15, 2014. (Pages 251-252)

The report also states:

Report on Aegis Ashore Missile Defense Test Complex

The committee directs the Director of the Missile Defense Agency, in coordination with the Commander, U.S. Pacific Command and the Commander, U.S. Strategic Command, to submit a report to the congressional defense committees not later than September 1, 2014, on the requirements and value of converting the Aegis Ashore Missile Defense Test Complex at the Pacific Missile Range Facility from a test and evaluation center to a permanent facility capable of continuous operations.

The report shall include the following:

(1) A description of manpower requirements associated with staffing the facility for continuous operations.

(2) A description of the safety mitigation strategies associated with permanent, continuous operations.

(3) A description of operational impacts at the Pacific Missile Range Facility complex.

(4) Anticipated operations and sustainment costs.

(5) A description of operational benefits and impacts of conversion to a permanent facility.

For the report described, the Director of the Missile Defense Agency shall include a consideration of the following:

(1) Technical feasibility.

(2) Cost, cost effectiveness, and affordability.

(3) Schedule considerations.

(4) Capacity to respond to changes in future threat evolution. (Page 305)

The report also states:

Standard Missile 3 Block IB

The committee is concerned by the reduction in funding for the Standard Missile 3 (SM–3) program in fiscal year 2015 and across the Future Years Defense Program (FYDP). After demonstrating success in five of five intercepts in 2013 and with a Full Rate Production decision planned for fall 2014, the Department now has reduced programmed quantities each year to fewer than were funded in fiscal year 2014 in Low Rate Initial Production. The committee believes such a reduction injects inefficiency into the production line and that inefficiency may unnecessarily increase the per unit cost of these interceptors.

At the same time, the committee is not aware of any diminishment in requirements by the combatant commanders for these interceptors. The committee supports the funding requested in the budget submission for Advanced Procurement to support long-lead time requirements for these missiles. The committee also supports the likely request in the fiscal year 2016 budget request for multiyear procurement authority for these missile interceptors. The committee believes that a successful negotiation between the Missile Defense Agency and its contractors could drive down the per unit cost of these interceptors and increase the available quantities to the warfighter.

The committee directs the Director, Missile Defense Agency to provide a briefing to the House Committee on Armed Services not later than October 1, 2014, on the sufficiency of current and programmed inventory of SM–3 missiles to meet combatant commander requirements, the number of Requests for Forces received from combatant commanders in 2012–13 for SM–3 interceptors, and the shortfall in interceptors in each year of the FYDP. (Page 312)

House (Floor Action)

On May 21, 2014, as part of its consideration of H.R. 4435, the House agreed to by voice vote H.Amdt. 688, an en bloc amendment consisting of several amendments printed in H.Rept. 113-460 of May 21 (legislative day, May 20), 2014, a report providing for further consideration of

H.R. 4435. One of these was amendment number 159 from H.Rept. 113-60, which increased by $99 million the amount authorized for Aegis BMD (line 30), and identified as offsets a $75.3 million reduction to the amount authorized in the Aircraft Procurement, Army, appropriation account for the Aerial Common Sensor (line 003) and a $23.7 million reduction to the amount authorized in the Procurement, Marine Corps, appropriation account for the RQ-21 Unmanned Aerial System (line 023).

Senate

The Senate Armed Services Committee, in its report (S.Rept. 113-176 of June 2, 2014) on S. 2410, makes the funding recommendations shown in **Table 5**.

Section 1612 of S. 2410 as reported states:

> SEC. 1612. REGIONAL BALLISTIC MISSILE DEFENSE.
>
> (a) Sense of Congress- It is the sense of Congress that--
>
> (1) the regional ballistic missile capabilities of countries such as Iran and North Korea pose a serious and growing threat to United States forward deployed forces, allies, and partner countries;
>
> (2) given this growing threat, it is a high priority for the United States to develop, test, and deploy effective regional missile defense capabilities to provide the commanders of the geographic combatant commands with capabilities to meet their operational requirements, and for United States allies and partners to improve their regional missile defense capabilities;
>
> (3) the United States and its North Atlantic Treaty Organization (NATO) partners should continue the development, testing, and implementation of Phases 2 and 3 of the European Phased Adaptive Approach, to defend United States forward deployed forces, allies, and partners in the North Atlantic Treaty Organization in Europe against the growing regional missile capability of Iran;
>
> (4) the United States should continue efforts to improve regional missile defense capabilities in the Middle East, including its close cooperation with Israel and its efforts with countries of the Gulf Cooperation Council, in order to improve regional security against the growing regional missile capabilities of Iran; and
>
> (5) the United States should continue to work closely with its allies in Asia, particularly Japan, South Korea, and Australia, to improve regional missile defense capabilities against the growing threat of North Korean ballistic missiles.
>
> (b) Report Required- Not later than 180 days after the date of the enactment of this Act, the Secretary of Defense shall submit to the congressional defense committees a report setting forth the status and progress of efforts to improve United States regional missile defense capabilities in Europe, the Middle East, and in the Asia-Pacific region, including efforts and cooperation by allies and partner countries.
>
> (c) Elements- The report required in subsection (b) shall include the following:

(1) A description of the status of implementation of the European Phased Adaptive Approach, including the status of efforts to develop, test, and deploy the capabilities planned for Phases 2 and 3 of the European Phased Adaptive Approach.

(2) A description of the status of efforts to improve the regional missile defense capabilities of the United States and the Gulf Cooperation Council countries in the Middle East against regional missile threats from Iran, including progress toward, and benefits of, multilateral cooperation and data sharing among the Gulf Cooperation Council countries for multilateral integrated air and missile defense against threats from Iran.

(3) A description of the progress of the United States and its allies in the Asia-Pacific region, particularly Japan, South Korea, and Australia, to improve regional missile defense capabilities against missile threats from North Korea.

(4) A description of the degree of coordination among the commanders of the geographic combatant commands for integrated missile defense planning and operations, including obstacles and opportunities to improving such coordination and integrated capabilities.

(5) A description of the phased and adaptive elements of United States regional missile defense approaches tailored to the specific regional requirements in the areas of responsibility of the United States Central Command and the United States Pacific Command, including the role of missile defense capabilities of United States allies and partners in each region.

(6) A summary of the regional missile defense risk assessment and priorities of the commanders of the geographic combatant commands.

(7) Such other matters as the Secretary considers appropriate.

(d) Form- The report required by subsection (b) shall be submitted in unclassified form, but may include a classified annex.

Regarding Section 1612, S.Rept. 113-176 states:

Regional ballistic missile defense (sec. 1612)

The committee recommends a provision that would express the sense of Congress on the importance of effective regional missile defenses to protect U.S. forward deployed forces, allies, and partner countries against the growing threat of regional ballistic missiles, particularly from Iran and North Korea, to Europe, the Middle East, and the Asia-Pacific region. The provision would require the Secretary of Defense to provide a report on the status and progress of efforts to improve regional missile defense capabilities in these regions, including efforts and cooperation by allies and partner countries.

The Missile Defense Agency reports that the European Phased Adaptive Approach (EPAA) to missile defense is on track to deploy the Phase 2 Aegis Ashore site in Romania in 2015 and the Phase 3 Aegis Ashore site in Poland by the end of 2018. These capabilities are intended to increase the defensive coverage of the North Atlantic Treaty Organization area of Europe against increasingly capable and numerous Iranian missiles. The committee supports the continued development, testing, and implementation of Phases 2 and 3 of the EPAA, and believes these capabilities will be important components of regional European security.

The committee notes that the United States is working with its Gulf Cooperation Council partner nations to improve regional air and missile defense capabilities, including data sharing and multilateral cooperation. The committee believes that such multilateral cooperation would enhance regional security and would provide significant improvements beyond national and bi-national capabilities. The committee encourages the Department of Defense (DOD) to make such multilateral air and missile defense cooperation a regional security priority.

The committee notes the significant missile defense cooperation with Japan, including the co-development of the Standard Missile-3 Block IIA interceptor, and believes this cooperation is an important element of the allied response to North Korea's regional missile capabilities. The committee encourages DOD to continue working with other allies and partners in the region, particularly including South Korea and Australia, to enhance protection against North Korean regional missile capabilities.

The committee notes that U.S. regional missile defense capabilities in each of these regions would be enhanced by increased interoperability and coordination among the geographic combatant commands and the capabilities under their control, and encourages DOD to take steps to maximize such interoperability and coordination. (Pages 217-218)

Appendix A. Aegis BMD Flight Tests

Summary of Test Flights

Table A-1 presents a DOD summary of Aegis BMD flight tests since January 2002. As shown in the table, DOD states that since January 2002, the Aegis BMD system has achieved 25 successful exo-atmospheric intercepts in 31 attempts using the SM-3 missile (including 3 successful intercepts in 4 attempts by Japanese Aegis ships), and 3 successful endo-atmospheric intercepts in 3 attempts using the SM-2 Block IV missile, making for a combined total of 28 successful intercepts in 34 attempts.

In addition, on February 20, 2008, a BMD-capable Aegis cruiser operating northwest of Hawaii used a modified version of the Aegis BMD system to shoot down an inoperable U.S. surveillance satellite that was in a deteriorating orbit—an operation called Burnt Frost. Including this intercept in the count increases the totals to 26 successful exo-atmospheric intercepts in 32 attempts using the SM-3 missile, and 29 successful exo- and endo-atmospheric intercepts in 35 attempts using both SM-3 and SM-2 Block IV missiles.

Table A-1. Aegis BMD Flight Tests Since January 2002

Date	Country	Name of flight test	Target	Successful?	Cumulative successes	Cumulative attempts
Exo-atmospheric (using SM-3 missile)						
1/25/02	US	FM-2	Unitary TTV short-range target	Yes	1	1
6/13/02	US	FM-3	Unitary TTV short-range target	Yes	2	2
11/21/02	US	FM-4	Unitary TTV short-range target	Yes	3	3
6/18/03	US	FM-5	Unitary TTV short-range target	No	3	4
12/11/03	US	FM-6	Unitary TTV medium-range target	Yes	4	5
2/24/05	US	FTM 04-1 (FM-7)	Unitary TTV short-range target	Yes	5	6
11/17/05	US	FTM 04-2 (FM-8)	Separating medium-range target	Yes	6	7
6/22/06	US	FTM 10	Separating medium-range target	Yes	7	8
12/7/06	US	FTM 11	Unitary TTV short-range target	No	7	9
4/26/07	US	FTM 11 Event 4	Unitary ARAV-A short-range target	Yes	8	10
6/22/07	US	FTM 12	Separating medium-range target	Yes	9	11
8/31/07	US	FTM-11a	Classified	Yes	10	12
11/6/07	US	FTM 13	Unitary ARAV-A short-range target	Yes	11	13
			Unitary ARAV-A short-range target	Yes	12	14
12/17/07	Japan	JFTM-1	Separating medium-range target	Yes	13	15
11/1/08	US	Pacific Blitz	Short-range target	Yes	14	16
			Short-range target	No	14	17
11/19/08	Japan	JFTM-2	Separating medium-range target	No	14	18
7/30/09	US	FTM-17	Unitary ARAV-A short-range target	Yes	15	19
10/27/09	Japan	JFTM-3	Separating medium-range target	Yes	16	20
10/28/10	Japan	JFTM-4	Separating medium-range target	Yes	17	21
4/14/11	US	FTM-15	LV-2 intermediate range target	Yes	18	22
9/1/11	US	FTM-16	Short-range target	No	18	23
5/9/12	US	FTM-16 E2a	Unitary ARAV-A short-range target	Yes	19	24
6/26/12	US	FTM-18	Separating medium-range target	Yes	20	25
10/25/12	US	FTI-01	Short-range target	No	20	26
2/12/13	US	FTM-20	Unitary medium-range target	Yes	21	27
5/15/13	US	FTM-19	Separating short-range target	Yes	22	28
9/10/13	US	FTO-01	Medium-range target	Yes	23	29
9/18/13	US	FTM-21	Complex separating short-range target	Yes	24	30
10/3/13	US	FTM-22	Medium-range target	Yes	25	31
Endo-atmospheric (using SM-2 missile)						
5/24/06	US	Pacific Pheonix	Unitary short-range target	Yes	1	1
6/5/08	US	FTM-14	Unitary short-range target	Yes	2	2
3/26/09	US	Stellar Daggers	Short-range target	Yes	3	3
Combined total for exo- and endo-atmospheric above tests					28	34

Source: Table adapted from table presented in MDA fact sheet, "Aegis Ballistic Missile Defense Testing," accessed on May 17, 2013, at http://www.mda.mil/global/documents/pdf/aegis_tests.pdf.

Notes: **TTV** is target test vehicle; **ARAV** is Aegis Readiness Assessment Vehicle. In addition to the flight tests shown above, there was a successful use of an SM-3 on February 20, 2008, to intercept an inoperative U.S. satellite—an operation called Burnt Frost. Including this intercept in the count increases the totals to 26 successful exo-atmospheric intercepts in 32 attempts using the SM-3 missile, and 29 successful exo- and endo-atmospheric intercepts in 35 attempts using both SM-3 and SM-2 Block IV missiles.

May 2010 Criticism of Claimed Successes in Flight Tests

In a May 2010 magazine article and supplementary white paper, two professors with scientific backgrounds—George Lewis and Theodore Postol—criticized DOD claims of successes in Aegis (and other DOD) BMD flight tests, arguing that

> the Defense Department's own test data show that, in combat, the vast majority of "successful" SM-3 experiments would have failed to destroy attacking warheads. The data also show potential adversaries how to defeat both the SM-3 and the GMD [ground-based missile defense] systems, which share the same serious flaws that can be readily exploited by adversaries.[44]

The criticisms made by Lewis and Postol were reported in a May 18, 2010, *New York Times* article.[45] In response to the criticisms and the *New York Times* article, MDA issued a press release and other information defending the flight tests and arguing that the criticisms are based on inaccurate or incomplete information.[46]

Details on Selected Exo-Atmospheric (SM-3) Flight Tests Since June 2006

June 22, 2006, Test. This was the first test to use the 3.6 version of the Aegis BMD system.[47]

December 7, 2006, Test. This was the first unsuccessful flight test since June 2003. MDA stated that the ninth test

> was not completed due to an incorrect system setting aboard the Aegis-class cruiser USS Lake Erie prior to the launch of two interceptor missiles from the ship. The incorrect configuration prevented the fire control system aboard the ship from launching the first of the two interceptor missiles. Since a primary test objective was a near-simultaneous launch of two missiles against two different targets, the second interceptor missile was intentionally not launched.
>
> The planned test was to involve the launch of a Standard Missile 3 against a ballistic missile target and a Standard Missile 2 against a surrogate aircraft target. The ballistic missile target was launched from the Pacific Missile Range Facility, Kauai, Hawaii and the aircraft target was launched from a Navy aircraft. The USS Lake Erie (CG 70), USS Hopper (DDG 70) and

---

[44] George N. Lewis and Theodore A. Postol, "A Flawed and Dangerous U.S. Missile Defense Plan," *Arms Control Today*, May 2010: 24-32. The quoted passage appears on p. 26. The associated white paper is George N. Lewis and Theodore A. Postol, *A Technically Detailed Description of Flaws in the SM-3 and GMD Missile Defense Systems Revealed by the Defense Department's Ballistic Missile Test Data*, May 3, 2010, 13 pp.

[45] William J. Broad and David E. Sanger, "Review Cites Flaws In U.S. Antimissile Program," *New York Times*, May 18, 2010: 1.

[46] Missile Defense Agency news release entitled "Missile Defense Agency Responds to New York Times Article," 10-News-0005, May 18, 2010; Missile Defense Agency, *Missile Defense Agency Response to Request for Information, Standard Missile – 3 Interceptor Testing*, May 18, 2010, 2 pp.; Missile Defense Agency, *Missile Defense Agency Response to Request for Information, Response to New York Times May 18, 2010, Article Regarding SM-3 Testing*, May 18, 2010, 3 pp.; Richard Lehner, "Missile Defense Agerncy Responds to New York Times Article," *DOD Live* (http://www.dodlive mil), May 18, 2010; Transcript of Department of Defense Bloggers Roundtable With Richard Lehner, Spokesman, Missile Defense Agency (MDA), Subject: Standard Missile 3 Test Program, May 18, 2010.

[47] Missile Defense Agency, "Missile Defense Test Results in Successful 'Hit To Kill' Intercept," June 22, 2006 (06-NEWS-0018).

---

the Royal Netherlands Navy frigate TROMP were all successful in detecting and tracking their respective targets. Both targets fell into the ocean as planned.

After a thorough review, the Missile Defense Agency and the U.S. Navy will determine a new test date.[48]

A news article about the ninth test stated:

"You can say it's seven of nine, rather than eight of nine," Missile Defense Agency spokesman Chris Taylor said of the second failure in tests of the system by the agency and the Navy....

The drill was planned to demonstrate the Navy's ability to knock down two incoming missiles at once from the same ship.

"In a real world situation it is possible, maybe even probable, that in addition to engaging a ballistic missile threat that was launched, you may be engaging a surface action," said Joe Rappisi before the test. He is director for the Aegis Ballistic Missile Defense system at Lockheed Martin, the primary contractor for the program.

The test would have marked the first time a ship has shot down one target in space and another target in the air at the same time.

The test presented a greater challenge to the ship's crew and the ballistic missile defense system than previous tests, Rappisi said. The multiple target scenario is also closer to what sailors might actually face in battle.

The U.S. Pacific Fleet has been gradually installing missile surveillance and tracking technology on many of its destroyers and cruisers amid concerns about North Korea's long-range missile program.

It is also installing interceptor missiles on many of its ships, even as the technology to track and shoot down incoming missiles is being developed and perfected.

The Royal Netherlands Navy joined the tracking and monitoring off Kauai to see how its equipment works. The Dutch presence marked the first time a European ally has sent one of its vessels to participate in a U.S. ballistic missile defense test.[49]

A subsequent news article stated:

the test abort of the Aegis Ballistic Missile Defense system Dec. 7 resulted from human error, [MDA Director USAF Lt. Gen. Henry] Obering says.... Both the ballistic missile and aircraft targets launched as planned, but the first interceptor failed to fire because an operator had selected an incorrect setting for the test. Officials then aborted before the second could boost.

Aegis missile defense system tests are at a standstill until officials are able to identify an appropriate ballistic missile target. The one used Dec. 7 was the last of its kind, Obering says, leaving them empty handed in the near future.[50]

---

[48] Untitled Missile Defense Agency "For Your Information" statement dated December 7, 2006 (06-FYI-0090).

[49] David Briscoe, "Test Interceptor Missile Fails To Launch," *NavyTimes.com*, December 8, 2006.

Another article stated:

> Philip Coyle, a former head of the Pentagon's testing directorate, gives the Navy credit for "discipline and successes so far" in its sea-based ballistic missile defense testing program. Coyle is now a senior adviser at the Center for Defense Information.
>
> "The U.S. Navy has an enviable track record of successful flight intercept tests, and is making the most of its current, limited Aegis missile defense capabilities in these tests," Coyle told [*Inside the Navy*] Dec. 7.
>
> "Difficulties such as those that delayed the latest flight intercept attempt illustrate the complexity of the system, and how everything must be carefully orchestrated to achieve success," Coyle added. "Nevertheless, this particular setback won't take the Navy long to correct."[51]

April 26, 2007, Test. MDA states that this test:

> involved the simultaneous engagements of a ballistic missile "unitary" target (meaning that the target warhead and booster remain attached) and a surrogate hostile air target....
>
> The test demonstrated the [Aegis ship's] ability to engage a ballistic missile threat and defend itself from attack at the same time. The test also demonstrated the effectiveness of engineering, manufacturing, and mission assurance changes in the solid divert and attitude control system (SDACS) in the kinetic kill weapon. This was the first flight test of all the SM-3 Block IA's upgrades, previously demonstrated in ground tests.[52]

A press report on the test stated that the hostile air target was an anti-ship cruise missile. The article stated that the scenario for the test

> called for the [Aegis ship] to come under attack from a cruise missile fired by an enemy plane.... A Navy plane fired the cruise missile target used in the test.[53]

June 22, 2007, Test. MDA states that this test

> was the third intercept involving a separating target and the first time an Aegis BMD-equipped destroyer was used to launch the interceptor missile. The USS Decatur (DDG 73), using the operationally-certified Aegis Ballistic Missile Defense Weapon System (BMD 3.6) and the Standard Missile-3 (SM-3) Block IA missile successfully intercepted the target during its midcourse phase of flight....
>
> An Aegis cruiser, USS Port Royal (CG 73), a Spanish frigate, MÉNDEZ NÚÑEZ (F-104), and MDA's Terminal High Altitude Area Defense (THAAD) mobile ground-based radar also participated in the flight test. USS Port Royal used the flight test to support development

---

(...continued)

[50] Amy Butler, "GMD Trial Delayed Until Spring; Aegis Failure Human Error," *Aerospace Daily & Defense Report*, December 19, 2006.

[51] Zachary M. Peterson, "Sea-Based Missile Defense Test Fails Due To 'Incorrect Configuration,'" *Inside the Navy*, December 11, 2006.

[52] Missile Defense Agency, "Successful Sea-Based Missile Defense 'Hit to Kill' Intercept," April 26, 2007 (07-NEWS-0032).

[53] Audrey McAvoy, "Aegis Missile Test Successful," *NavyTimes.com*, April 27, 2007.

of the new Aegis BMD SPY-1B radar signal processor, collecting performance data on its increased target detection and discrimination capabilities. MÉNDEZ NÚÑEZ, stationed off Kauai, performed long-range surveillance and track operations as a training event to assess the future capabilities of the F-100 Class. The THAAD radar tracked the target and exchanged tracking data with the Aegis BMD cruiser.

This event marked the third time that an allied military unit participated in a U.S. Aegis BMD test, with warships from Japan and the Netherlands participating in earlier tests.[54]

August 31, 2007, Test. MDA has publicly noted the occurrence of this test and the fact that it resulted in a successful intercept,[55] but states that the details about the test are classified.[56] MDA does not appear to have issued a news release about this flight test following the completion of the test, as it has for other Aegis BMD flight tests.[57]

November 6, 2007, Test. MDA states that this test involved:

> a multiple simultaneous engagement involving two ballistic missile targets.... For the first time, the operationally realistic test involved two unitary "non-separating" targets, meaning that the target's warheads did not separate from their booster rockets....
>
> At approximately 6:12 p.m. Hawaii Standard Time (11:12 p.m. EST), a target was launched from the Pacific Missile Range Facility (PMRF), Barking Sands, Kauai, Hawaii. Moments later, a second, identical target was launched from the PMRF. The USS Lake Erie's Aegis BMD Weapon System detected and tracked the targets and developed fire control solutions.
>
> Approximately two minutes later, the USS Lake Erie's crew fired two SM-3 missiles, and two minutes later they successfully intercepted the targets outside the earth's atmosphere more than 100 miles above the Pacific Ocean and 250 miles northwest of Kauai....
>
> A Japanese destroyer also participated in the flight test. Stationed off Kauai and equipped with the certified 3.6 Aegis BMD weapon system, the guided missile destroyer JS Kongo performed long-range surveillance and tracking exercises. The Kongo used the test as a training exercise in preparation for the first ballistic missile intercept test by a Japanese ship planned for later this year. This event marked the fourth time an allied military unit participated in a U.S. Aegis BMDS test.[58]

---

[54] Missile Defense Agency, "Sea-Based Missile Defense 'Hit to Kill' Intercept Achieved," June 22, 2007 (07-NEWS-0037).

[55] See for example, slide 8 in the 20-slide briefing entitled "Ballistic Missile Defense Program Overview For The Congressional Breakfast Seminar Series," dated June 20, 2008, presented by Lieutenant General Trey Obering, USAF, Director, Missile Defense Agency. Source for briefing: *InsideDefense.com* (subscription required). Each slide in the briefing includes a note indicating that it was approved by MDA for public release on June 13, 2008. Slide 8 lists Aegis BMD midcourse flight tests conducted since September 2005, including a test on August 31, 2007. The slide indicates with a check mark that the flight test was successful. A success in this test is also needed to for the total number of successful intercepts to match the reported figure.

[56] An e-mail from MDA to CRS dated June 30, 2008, states that the flight test "was a hit to kill intercept test but details about the test are classified."

[57] MDA's website, when accessed on June 30, 2008, did not show a news release issued on of soon after August 31, 2007, that discusses this test.

[58] Missile Defense Agency, "Sea-Based Missile Defense "Hit to Kill" Intercept Achieved," November 6, 2007 (07-NEWS-0051).

December 17, 2007, Test. In this flight test, a BMD-capable Japanese Aegis destroyer used an SM-3 Block IA missile to successfully intercept a ballistic missile target in a flight test off the coast of Hawaii. It was the first time that a non-U.S. ship had intercepted a ballistic missile using the Aegis BMD system.[59]

November 1, 2008, Test. This flight test was reportedly the first U.S. Navy Aegis BMD flight test conducted by the Navy, without oversight by MDA. The test involved two Aegis ships, each attempting to intercept a ballistic missile. The SM-3 fired by the first Aegis ship successfully intercepted its target, but the SM-3 fired by the second Aegis ship did not intercept its target. A press release from the U.S. Third Fleet (the Navy's fleet for the Eastern Pacific) states that

> Vice Adm. Samuel J. Locklear, Commander, U.S. Third Fleet announced today the successful Navy intercept of a ballistic missile target over the Pacific Ocean during Fleet Exercise Pacific Blitz. This was the first Fleet operational firing to employ the Standard Missile-3 (SM-3) against a ballistic missile target. Command and control of this mission resided with Commander, U.S. Third Fleet, based in San Diego, Calif.

> Pearl Harbor-based Aegis destroyers, USS Paul Hamilton (DDG 60) and USS Hopper (DDG 70), which have been upgraded to engage ballistic missiles, fired SM-3 missiles at separate targets. During this event, a short-range ballistic missile target was launched from the Pacific Missile Range Facility (PMRF), Barking Sands, Kauai, Hawaii. Upon detecting and tracking the target, USS Paul Hamilton, launched a SM-3 missile, resulting in a direct-hit intercept. Following USS Paul Hamilton's engagement, PMRF launched another target. USS Hopper successfully detected, tracked and engaged the target. The SM-3 followed a nominal trajectory, however intercept was not achieved. Extensive analysis of the flight mission will be used to improve the deployed Aegis BMD system.[60]

November 19, 2008, Test. This was the second Japanese flight test, and involved a single ballistic missile target. The test did not result in a successful intercept. MDA states that

> Rear Admiral Tomohisa Takei, Director General of Operations and Plans, for the Japanese Maritime Staff Office (MSO), Japan Maritime Self Defense Force (JMSDF), and Lt. General Henry "Trey" Obering, United States Missile Defense Agency director, announced the completion today of a cooperative sea-based Aegis Ballistic Missile Defense intercept flight test off the coast of Kauai in Hawaii. The event, designated Japan Flight Test Mission 2 (JFTM-2), marked the second attempt by an Allied naval ship to intercept a ballistic missile target with the sea-based midcourse engagement capability provided by Aegis Ballistic Missile Defense. Target performance, interceptor missile launch and flyout, and operation of the Aegis Weapon System by the crew were successful, but an intercept was not achieved.

> The JFTM-2 was a test of the newest engagement capability of the Aegis Ballistic Missile Defense configuration of the recently upgraded Japanese destroyer, JS CHOKAI (DDG-176). At approximately 4:21 pm (HST), 11:21 am (Tokyo time) a ballistic missile target was launched from the Pacific Missile Range Facility, Barking Sands, Kauai, Hawaii. JS CHOKAI crew members detected and tracked the target using an advanced on-board radar.

[59] John Liang, "Japanese Destroyer Shoots Down Ballistic Missile Test Target," *Inside Missile Defense*, December 19, 2007; "Japanese Aegis Destroyer Wins Test By Killing Target Missile With SM-3 Interceptor," *Defense Daily*, December 18, 2007; Reuters, "Japanese Ship Downs Missile In Pacific Test," *New York Times*, December 18, 2007: 8; Audrey McAvoy, "Japan Intercepts Missile In Test Off Hawaii," NavyTimes.com, December 17, 2007.

[60] Commander, U.S. Third Fleet, Public Affairs Office, press release 23-08, dated November 1, 2008, entitled "Navy Intercepts Ballistic Missile Target in Fleet Exercise Pacific Blitz." See also Dave Ahearn, "One of Two Missiles Hit In Aegis Test; Navy For First Time Runs Test Instead of MDA," *Defense Daily*, November 4, 2008: 1-2.

The Aegis Weapon System then developed a fire control solution, and at approximately 4:24 pm (HST), 11:24 am (Tokyo time) on Nov 20, a single Standard Missile -3 (SM-3) Block IA was launched. Approximately two minutes later, the SM-3 failed to intercept the target. There is no immediate explanation for the failed intercept attempt. More information will be available after a thorough investigation. The JS CHOKAI crew performance was excellent in executing the mission. JFTM-2 was the second time that a Japanese ship was designated to launch the interceptor missile, a major milestone in the growing cooperation between Japan and the U.S.[61]

A November 21, 2008, press report states that

An Aegis ballistic missile defense (BMD) test by the Japanese destroyer Chokai (DDG-176) ended in failure when the Standard Missile-3 Block 1A interceptor lost track of the target missile in the final seconds before a planned hit-to-kill.

The Chokai and its crew performed well throughout the test, and the SM-3 also performed flawlessly through its first three stages, according to Rear Adm. Brad Hicks, the U.S. Navy Aegis ballistic missile defense program director. He spoke with several reporters in a teleconference around midnight ET Wednesday-Thursday, after the test in the area of the Pacific Missile Range Facility, Barking Sands, Kauai, Hawaii.

This was the second Aegis BMD test failure in less than a month.

These latest two failures come as some Democrats in Congress are poised to cut spending on missile defense programs when they convene next year to consider the Missile Defense Agency budget for the fiscal year ending Sept. 30, 2010....

Still, in the coming money debates next year, missile defense advocates will be able to point out that even including the Hopper and Chokai failures, the record for the Aegis tests is an overwhelming 16 successful hits demolishing target missiles out of 20 attempts.

Those successes included the first Japanese attempt. The Japanese destroyer Kongo (DDG-173) successfully used its SM-3 interceptor to kill a target missile. The difference in tests is that the Kongo crew was advised beforehand when the target missile would be launched, while the Chokai crew wasn't....

[Hicks] said a board will be convened to examine why the latest test failed. Hicks declined to speculate on why the SM-3 interceptor missed the target. "I'm confident we'll find out the root cause" of the Chokai interceptor failure to score a hit, he said.

However, he was asked by *Space & Missile Defense Report* whether the prior SM-3 successes make it unlikely the Chokai failure stems from some basic design flaw in all SM-3s, and whether it is more likely that the Chokai SM-3 failed because of some flaw or glitch in just that one interceptor.

Hicks said that is likely.

"Obviously, we believe this is hopefully related to this one interceptor," and doesn't reflect any basic design flaw in the SM-3 interceptors, he said.

---

[61] Missile Defense Agency press release 08-News-0087, dated November 19, 2008, entitled "Japan/U.S. Missile Defense Flight Test Completed."

The Chokai test failure cost Japan a $55 million loss, he said, adding, "It wasn't cheap.".....

In the Chokai test, the target missile was launched from Barking Sands, and about three minutes later the Chokai crew had spotted the target, the Aegis system had developed a tracking and hit solution, and the SM-3 interceptor was launched.

The first, second and third stages of the interceptor performed nominally, without problems, but then came the fourth stage. The nosecone components opened to expose the kill vehicle area, and somehow the program to track the target missile failed.

"It lost track," Hicks said, only seconds before the hit would have been achieved.

If the kill had occurred, it would have been about 100 nautical miles (roughly 115 statute miles) above Earth, and some 250 miles away from Barking Sands, Hicks said.

It took the interceptor about two minutes flight time to reach the near miss with the target missile.

Meanwhile, the Hamilton was nearby watching the test. The Hamilton Aegis system successfully spotted and tracked the target, and developed a simulated solution and simulated interceptor launch that, if it had been real, would have resulted in a successful hit on the target, Hicks said. The Hamilton didn't cue the Chokai, however. "It was strictly Chokai's engagement," Hicks said.[62]

July 30, 2009, Test. MDA states that

In conjunction with the Missile Defense Agency (MDA), U.S. Pacific Fleet ships and crews successfully conducted the latest Aegis Ballistic Missile Defense (BMD) at-sea firing event on July 30. During this event, entitled Stellar Avenger, the Aegis BMD-equipped ship, USS Hopper (DDG 70), detected, tracked, fired and guided a Standard Missile -3 (SM-3) Block (Blk) IA to intercept a sub-scale short range ballistic missile. The target was launched from the Kauai Test Facility, co-located on the Pacific Missile Range Facility (PMRF), Barking Sands, Kauai. It was the 19th successful intercept in 23 at-sea firings, for the Aegis BMD Program, including the February 2008 destruction of the malfunctioning satellite above the earth's atmosphere. Stellar Avenger was part of the continual evaluation of the certified and fielded Aegis BMD system at-sea today.

At approximately 5:40 pm (HST), 11:40 pm (EDT), a target was launched from PMRF. Three U.S. Navy Aegis BMD-equipped ships, the cruiser, USS Lake Erie (CG 70) and destroyers USS Hopper (DDG 70) and USS O'Kane (DDG 77) detected and tracked the target with their SPY radars. Each developed fire control solutions. At 5:42 pm (HST), 11:42 pm (EDT) the crew of USS Hopper fired one SM-3 Blk IA missile. The USS Hopper's Aegis BMD Weapon System successfully guided the SM-3 to a direct body to body hit, approximately two minutes after leaving the ship. The intercept occurred about 100 miles above the Pacific Ocean. USS O'Kane conducted a simulated engagement of the target. USS Lake Erie, with its recently installed upgraded Aegis BMD 4.0.1 Weapons System, detected and tracked the same target.[63]

---

[62] Dave Ahearn, "Japanese Aegis Missile Defense Test Fails, But Aegis Record Is 16 Hits In 20 Tries," Defense Daily, November 21, 2008: 5-6.

[63] Missile Defense Agency press release 09-News-0015, dated July 31, 2009, entitled "Aegis Ballistic Missile Defense Test Successful."

A July 31, 2009, press report states:

> The test was the first Aegis BMD exercise to feature two versions of the software in a single event, according to Lisa Callahan, Lockheed's vice president for ballistic missile defense programs.
>
> A goal of the exercises was to test the Aegis system's ability to discern all the different parts and pieces of a ballistic missile, Nick Bucci, Lockheed's director for Aegis BMD development programs, told reporters July 29 during a pre-exercise conference call.
>
> Three more flight tests this fall will further test the system's discrimination capabilities, Bucci added, with each test becoming more complex. The last test will "be against a pretty darn complex target," he said.
>
> The July 30 tests also validated fixes put in place after a BMD test last November involving a missile launched from the Aegis BMD Japanese destroyer Chokai failed to intercept its target, according to MDA spokesman Chris Taylor. The improvements—which were successful in the most recent test—involved fixes to the Solid Divert Attitude Control System.
>
> The Chokai is the second of four Japanese Aegis ships being upgraded with BMD capability. A third ship, the Myoko, is scheduled to carry out a BMD test this fall.[64]

An August 3, 2009, press report states:

> This test was added to the schedule to evaluate changes made after last year's failed attempt to intercept a target with an SM-3 Block IA launched by a Japanese Aegis-equipped ship .... After the Nov. 19 test, MDA officials said, "Target performance, interceptor missile launch and flyout, and operation of the Aegis Weapon System by the crew were successful, but an intercept was not achieved."
>
> A root cause has not been identified, and an MDA spokesman did not say whether fixes have been made to hardware or operational procedures resulting from the failure review. It is also unclear why a subscale target was used in the July 30 trial.[65]

An August 4, 2009, press report states:

> [Rear Admiral Alan "Brad" Hicks, Aegis/SM-3 program manager for MDA], said that a November [2008] failure of an SM-3 Block IA... during a flight-test was attributable to poor adherence to processes on Raytheon's assembly line in Tucson, Ariz.
>
> This was isolated to that missile, and it was the result of perturbations to the build process encountered when shifting from development to production operations.
>
> During the November test, a Japanese Aegis-equipped ship fired the interceptor and it flew "perfectly," Hicks said. In the endgame, a failure of the divert and attitude control system on the unitary kill vehicle led to a miss.
>
> The July 30 demonstration using a U.S. ship "restored confidence" for the Japanese that the miss last fall was an isolated incident, he says.[66]

---

[64] Christopher P. Cavas, "Aegis BMD Test Successful," *DefenseNews.com*, July 31, 2009.

[65] Amy Butler, "SM-3 Scores Hit After Fixes Implemented," *Aerospace Daily & Defense Report*, August 3, 2009: 5.

October 27, 2009, Test. This was the third Japanese flight test, and it involved a single ballistic missile target. MDA states that

> The Japan Maritime Self-Defense Force (JMSDF) and the United States Missile Defense Agency (MDA) announced the successful completion of an Aegis Ballistic Missile Defense (BMD) intercept flight test, in cooperation with the U.S. Navy, off the coast of Kauai in Hawaii. The event, designated Japan Flight Test Mission 3 (JFTM-3), marked the third time that a JMSDF ship has successfully engaged a ballistic missile target, including two successful intercepts, with the sea-based midcourse engagement capability provided by Aegis BMD.

> The JFTM-3 test event verified the newest engagement capability of the Japan Aegis BMD configuration of the recently upgraded Japanese destroyer, JS MYOKO (DDG-175). At approximately 6:00pm (HST), 1:00 pm Tokyo time on Oct 28, a separating, medium-range ballistic missile target was launched from the Pacific Missile Range Facility, Barking Sands, Kauai, Hawaii. JS MYOKO crew members detected and tracked the target. The Aegis Weapon System then developed a fire control solution and, at approximately 6:04pm (HST), 1:04 pm Tokyo time a Standard Missile-3 (SM-3) Block IA interceptor missile was launched. Approximately 3 minutes later, the SM-3 successfully intercepted the target approximately 100 miles above the Pacific Ocean. JFTM-3 is a significant milestone in the growing cooperation between Japan and the U.S. in the area of missile defense.

> Also participating in the test, were the Pearl Harbor-based USS Lake Erie (CG 70) and USS Paul Hamilton (DDG 60) which detected and tracked the target and conducted a simulated engagement.[67]

October 28, 2010, Test. This was the fourth Japanese flight test, and it involved a single ballistic missile target. MDA states that

> The Japan Maritime Self-Defense Force (JMSDF) and the United States Missile Defense Agency (MDA) announced the successful completion of an Aegis Ballistic Missile Defense (BMD) intercept flight test, in cooperation with the U.S. Navy, off the coast of Kauai in Hawaii.

> The event marked the fourth time that a JMSDF ship has engaged a ballistic missile target, including three successful intercepts, with the sea-based midcourse engagement capability provided by Aegis BMD.

> The JFTM-4 test event verified the newest engagement capability of the Japan Aegis BMD configuration of the recently upgraded Japanese destroyer, JS KIRISHIMA. At approximately 5:06 p.m. (HST), 12:06 p.m. Tokyo time on Oct. 29, 2010, a separating 1,000 km class ballistic missile target was launched from the Pacific Missile Range Facility at Barking Sands, Kauai, Hawaii.

(...continued)

[66] Amy Butler, "SM-3 Upgrade Program Cost Increases," *Aerospace Daily & Defense Report*, August 4, 2009: 1-2. See also Dan Taylor, "Navy Conducts Aegis BMD Test, New Baseline System Participates," *Inside the Navy*, August 3, 2009; Daniel Wasserbly, "US Aegis BMD System Achieves Trial Success," *Jane's Defence Weekly*, August 5, 2009: 8.

[67] Missile Defense Agency press release 09-News-0021, dated October 28, 2009, entitled "Japan/U.S. Missile Defense Flight Test Successful." See also Christopher P. Cavas, "Japanese Destroyer Conducts Successful BMD Test," *NavyTimes.com*, October 28, 2009; and Amy Butler and Michael Bruno, "SM-3 Scores Hit In Japanese Test," *Aerospace Daily & Defense Report*," October 29, 2009: 3.

JS KIRISHIMA crew members detected and tracked the target. The Aegis Weapon System then developed a fire control solution and launched a Standard Missile -3 (SM-3) Block IA missile. Approximately three minutes later, the SM-3 successfully intercepted the target approximately 100 miles above the Pacific Ocean. JFTM-4 is a significant milestone in the growing cooperation between Japan and the U.S. in the area of missile defense.

Also participating in the test was USS LAKE ERIE and USS RUSSELL, Aegis ships which cooperated to detect, track and conduct a simulated intercept engagement against the same target.[68]

April 15, 2011, Test. MDA states that this flight test "was the most challenging test to date, as it was the first Aegis BMD version 3.6.1 intercept against an intermediate-range target (range 1,864 to 3,418 [statute] miles) and the first Aegis BMD 3.6.1 engagement relying on remote tracking data." MDA states that

> The Missile Defense Agency (MDA), U.S. Navy sailors aboard the Aegis destroyer USS O'KANE (DDG 77), and Soldiers from the 94th Army Air and Missile Defense Command operating from the 613th Air and Space Operations Center at Hickam Air Force Base, Hawaii, successfully conducted a flight test of the Aegis Ballistic Missile Defense (BMD) element of the nation's Ballistic Missile Defense System, resulting in the intercept of a separating ballistic missile target over the Pacific Ocean. This successful test demonstrated the capability of the first phase of the European Phased Adaptive Approach (EPAA) announced by the President in September, 2009.

> At 2:52 a.m. EDT (6:52 p.m. April 15 Marshall Island Time), an intermediate-range ballistic missile target was launched from the Reagan Test Site, located on Kwajalein Atoll in the Republic of the Marshall Islands, approximately 2,300 miles southwest of Hawaii. The target flew in a northeasterly direction towards a broad ocean area in the Pacific Ocean. Following target launch, a forward-based AN/TPY-2 X-band transportable radar, located on Wake Island, detected and tracked the threat missile. The radar sent trajectory information to the Command, Control, Battle Management, and Communications (C2BMC) system, which processed and transmitted remote target data to the USS O'KANE. The destroyer, located to the west of Hawaii, used the data to develop a fire control solution and launch the SM-3 Block IA missile approximately 11 minutes after the target was launched.

> As the IRBM target continued along its trajectory, the firing ship's AN/SPY-1 radar detected and acquired the ballistic missile target. The firing ship's Aegis BMD weapon system uplinked target track information to the SM-3 Block IA missile. The SM-3 maneuvered to a point in space as designated by the fire control solution and released its kinetic warhead. The kinetic warhead acquired the target, diverted into its path, and, using only force of a direct impact, destroyed the threat in a "hit-to-kill" intercept.

> During the test the C2BMC system, operated by Soldiers from the 94th Army Air and Missile Defense Command, received data from all assets and provided situational awareness of the engagement to U.S. Pacific Command, U.S. Northern Command and U.S. Strategic Command.

---

[68] Missile Defense Agency press release 10-News-0016, dated October 29, 2010, entitled "Joint Japan-U.S. Missile Defense Flight Test Successful." See also Marina Malenic, "Japanese Aegis Destroyer Successfully Completes Missile-Intercept Test," *Defense Daily*, November 1, 2010: 6.

The two demonstration Space Tracking and Surveillance Satellites (STSS), launched by MDA in 2009, successfully acquired the target missile, providing stereo "birth to death" tracking of the target.

Today's event, designated Flight Test Standard Missile-15 (FTM-15), was the most challenging test to date, as it was the first Aegis BMD version 3.6.1 intercept against an intermediate-range target (range 1,864 to 3,418 [statute] miles) and the first Aegis BMD 3.6.1 engagement relying on remote tracking data. The ability to use remote radar data to engage a threat ballistic missile greatly increases the battle space and defended area of the SM-3 missile.

Initial indications are that all components performed as designed. Program officials will spend the next several months conducting an extensive assessment and evaluation of system performance based upon telemetry and other data obtained during the test.[69]

September 1, 2011, Test. This flight test, which did not result in an intercept, was the first flight test of the SM-3 Block IB interceptor. MDA states that it

> was unable to achieve the planned intercept of a ballistic missile target during a test over the Pacific Ocean exercising the sea-based element of the Ballistic Missile Defense System (BMDS).
>
> At approximately 3:53 a.m. Hawaii Standard Time (9:53 a.m. EDT) a short-range ballistic missile target was launched from the U.S. Navy's Pacific Missile Range Facility on Kauai, Hawaii. Approximately 90 seconds later, a Standard Missile 3 (SM-3) Block 1B interceptor missile was launched from the cruiser USS LAKE ERIE (CG-70) but an intercept of the target was not achieved.
>
> This was the first flight test of the advanced SM-3 Block 1B interceptor missile. Program officials will conduct an extensive investigation to determine the cause of the failure to intercept.[70]

May 9, 2012, Test. MDA states that this flight test "was the first successful live fire intercept test of the SM-3 Block IB interceptor and the second-generation Aegis BMD 4.0.1 weapon system." MDA states that

> The Missile Defense Agency (MDA) and U.S. Navy sailors aboard the USS LAKE ERIE (CG 70) successfully conducted a flight test of the Aegis Ballistic Missile Defense (BMD) system, resulting in the first intercept of a short-range ballistic missile target over the Pacific Ocean by the Navy's newest Missile Defense interceptor, the Standard Missile – 3 (SM-3) Block IB.
>
> At 8:18 p.m. Hawaiian Standard Time (2:18 a.m. EDT May 10) the target missile was launched from the Pacific Missile Range Facility, located on Kauai, Hawaii. The target flew on a northwesterly trajectory towards a broad ocean area of the Pacific Ocean. Following target launch, the USS LAKE ERIE detected and tracked the missile with its onboard

---

[69] Missile Defense Agency press release 11-News-0007, dated April 15, 2011, entitled "Sea-based Missile Defense Flight Test Results in Successful Intercept."

[70] Missile Defense Agency press release 11-News-0016, dated September 1, 2011, entitled "Sea-Based Missile Defense Test Conducted." See also Amy Butler, "Upgraded Ballistic Missile Killer Fizzles In First Flight Test," *Aerospace Daily & Defense Report*, September 2, 2011: 3; and Mike McCarthy, "Sea-Based Missile Defense Test Fails," *Defense Daily*, September 2, 2011: 2-3.

AN/SPY-1 radar. The ship, equipped with the second-generation Aegis BMD 4.0.1 weapon system, developed a fire control solution and launched the Standard Missile-3 (SM-3) Block IB interceptor.

The USS LAKE ERIE continued to track the target and sent trajectory information to the SM-3 Block IB interceptor in-flight. The SM-3 maneuvered to a point in space, as designated by the fire control solution, and released its kinetic warhead. The kinetic warhead acquired the target, diverted into its path, and, using only the force of a direct impact, engaged and destroyed the threat in a hit-to-kill intercept.

Today's event, designated Flight Test Standard Missile-16 (FTM-16) Event 2a, was the first successful live fire intercept test of the SM-3 Block IB interceptor and the second-generation Aegis BMD 4.0.1 weapon system. Previous successful intercepts were conducted with the Aegis BMD 3.6.1 weapon system and the SM-3 Block IA interceptor, which are currently operational on U.S. Navy ships deployed across the globe....

Initial indications are that all components performed as designed. Program officials will conduct an extensive assessment and evaluation of system performance based upon telemetry and other data obtained during the test.[71]

June 26, 2012, Test. MDA states that this flight test "was the second consecutive successful intercept test of the SM-3 Block IB missile and the second-generation Aegis BMD 4.0.1 weapon system." MDA states that

> The Missile Defense Agency (MDA) and U.S. Navy sailors in the USS LAKE ERIE (CG 70) successfully conducted a flight test of the Aegis Ballistic Missile Defense (BMD) system, resulting in the intercept of a separating ballistic missile target over the Pacific Ocean by the Navy's newest missile defense interceptor missile, the Standard Missile-3 (SM-3) Block IB.
>
> At 11:15 pm Hawaii Standard Time, June 26 (5:15 am EDT June 27), the target missile was launched from the Pacific Missile Range Facility, located on Kauai, Hawaii. The target flew on a northwesterly trajectory towards a broad ocean area of the Pacific Ocean. Following target launch, the USS LAKE ERIE detected and tracked the missile with its onboard AN/SPY-1 radar. The ship, equipped with the second-generation Aegis BMD 4.0.1 weapon system, developed a fire control solution and launched the SM-3 Block IB missile.
>
> The USS LAKE ERIE continued to track the target and sent trajectory information to the SM-3 Block IB missile in-flight. The SM-3 maneuvered to a point in space, as designated by the fire control solution, and released its kinetic warhead. The kinetic warhead acquired the target, diverted into its path, and, using only the force of a direct impact, engaged and destroyed the threat in a hit-to-kill intercept.
>
> Today's test event was the second consecutive successful intercept test of the SM-3 Block IB missile and the second-generation Aegis BMD 4.0.1 weapon system. The first successful SM-3 Block IB intercept occurred on May 9, 2012. Today's intercept is a critical accomplishment for the second phase of the President's European Phased Adaptive Approach consisting of the SM-3 Block IB interceptor employed in an Aegis Ashore system in Romania in 2015.

---

[71] Missile Defense Agency press release 12-News-0007, dated May 9, 2012, entitled "Second-Generation Aegis Ballistic Missile Defense System Completes Successful Intercept Flight Test."

Initial indications are that all components performed as designed resulting in a very accurate intercept.[72]

October 25, 2012, Test. MDA states that in this flight test,

> The Missile Defense Agency (MDA), U.S. Army soldiers from the 94th and 32nd Army Air and Missile Defense Command (AAMDC); U.S. Navy sailors aboard the USS FITZGERALD (DDG 62); and airmen from the 613th Air and Space Operations Center successfully conducted the largest, most complex missile defense flight test ever attempted resulting in the simultaneous engagement of five ballistic missile and cruise missile targets. An integrated air and ballistic missile defense architecture used multiple sensors and missile defense systems to engage multiple targets at the same time....
>
> The USS FITZGERALD successfully engaged a low flying cruise missile over water. The Aegis system also tracked and launched an SM-3 Block 1A interceptor against a Short-Range Ballistic Missile. However, despite indication of a nominal flight of the SM-3 Block 1A interceptor, there was no indication of an intercept of the SRBM.[73]

February 12, 2013, Test. MDA states that in this flight test,

> The Missile Defense Agency (MDA) and U.S. Navy sailors aboard the USS LAKE ERIE (CG 70) successfully conducted a flight test of the Aegis Ballistic Missile Defense (BMD) system, resulting in the intercept of a medium-range ballistic missile target over the Pacific Ocean by a Standard Missile-3 (SM-3) Block IA guided missile.
>
> At 11:10 p.m. HST (4:10 a.m. EST) a unitary medium-range ballistic missile target was launched from the Pacific Missile Range Facility, on Kauai, Hawaii. The target flew northwest towards a broad ocean area of the Pacific Ocean.
>
> The in-orbit Space Tracking and Surveillance System-Demonstrators (STSS-D) detected and tracked the target, and forwarded track data to the USS LAKE ERIE. The ship, equipped with the second-generation Aegis BMD weapon system, used Launch on Remote doctrine to engage the target.
>
> The ship developed a fire control solution from the STSS-D track and launched the SM-3 Block IA guided missile approximately five minutes after target launch. The SM-3 maneuvered to a point in space and released its kinetic warhead. The kinetic warhead acquired the target reentry vehicle, diverted into its path, and, using only the force of a direct impact, engaged and destroyed the target.
>
> Initial indications are that all components performed as designed. Program officials will assess and evaluate system performance based upon telemetry and other data obtained during the test.
>
> Today's event, designated Flight Test Standard Missile-20 (FTM-20), was a demonstration of the ability of space-based assets to provide mid-course fire control quality data to an

---

[72] Missile Defense Agency press release 12-News-0008, dated June 27, 2012, entitled "Second-Generation Aegis Ballistic Missile Defense System Completes Second Successful Intercept Flight Test."

[73] Missile Defense Agency press release 12-News-0011, dated October 25, 2012, entitled "Ballistic Missile Defense System Engages Five Targets Simultaneously During Largest Missile Defense Flight Test in History."

Aegis BMD ship, extending the battlespace, providing the ability for longer range intercepts and defense of larger areas.[74]

May 16, 2013, Test. MDA states that in this flight test,

> The Missile Defense Agency (MDA) and U.S. Navy sailors aboard the USS LAKE ERIE (CG-70) successfully conducted a flight test today of the Aegis Ballistic Missile Defense (BMD) system, resulting in the intercept of a separating ballistic missile target over the Pacific Ocean by the Aegis BMD 4.0 Weapon System and a Standard Missile-3 (SM-3) Block IB missile.
>
> At 5:25 p.m. (Hawaii Time, 11:25 p.m. EDT), May 15, a separating short-range ballistic missile target was launched from the Pacific Missile Range Facility, on Kauai, Hawaii. The target flew northwest towards a broad ocean area of the Pacific Ocean. Following target launch, the USS LAKE ERIE (CG-70) detected and tracked the missile with its onboard AN/SPY-1 radar. The ship, equipped with the second-generation Aegis BMD weapon system, developed a fire control solution and launched the SM-3 Block IB missile. The SM-3 maneuvered to a point in space based on guidance from Aegis BMD Weapons Systems and released its kinetic warhead. The kinetic warhead acquired the target reentry vehicle, diverted into its path, and, using only the force of a direct impact, engaged and destroyed the target.
>
> Initial indications are that all components performed as designed. Program officials will assess and evaluate system performance based upon telemetry and other data obtained during the test.
>
> This test exercised the latest version of the second-generation Aegis BMD Weapon System and Standard Missile, providing capability for engagement of longer-range and more sophisticated ballistic missiles.
>
> Last night's event, designated Flight Test Standard Missile-19 (FTM-19), was the third consecutive successful intercept test of the Aegis BMD 4.0 Weapon System and the SM-3 Block IB guided missile. Previous successful ABMD 4.0 SM-3 Block IB intercepts occurred on May 9, 2012 and June 26, 2012. Other Aegis BMD intercepts have employed the ABMD 3.6 and 4.0 with the SM-3 Block IA missile, which is currently operational on U.S. Navy ships deployed across the globe.[75]

September 10, 2013, Test. MDA states that in this flight test,

> The Missile Defense Agency (MDA), Ballistic Missile Defense System (BMDS) Operational Test Agency, Joint Functional Component Command for Integrated Missile Defense, and U.S. Pacific Command, in conjunction with U.S. Army soldiers from the Alpha Battery, 2nd Air Defense Artillery Regiment, U.S. Navy sailors aboard the guided missile destroyer USS Decatur (DDG-73), and U.S. Air Force airmen from the 613th Air and Operations Center

---

[74] Missile Defense Agency press release 13-News-0002, dated February 13, 2013, entitled "Aegis Ballistic Missile Defense Intercepts Target Using Space Tracking and Surveillance System-Demonstrators (STSS-D) Data." See also Troy Clarke, "Space-Based Sensors Star in "Stellar Eyes" Missile Defense Test," *Navy News Service*, February 13, 2013.

[75] Missile Defense Agency press release 13-News-0005, dated May 16, 2013, entitled "Aegis Ballistic Missile Defense System Completes Successful Intercept Flight Test." See also Mike McCarthy, "Aegis Missile Intercept Successful," *Defense Daily*, May 17, 2013: 7-8; and Amy Butler, "MDA Conducts Two Successful Flight Tests," *Aerospace Daily & Defense Report*, May 17, 2013: 3.

successfully conducted a complex missile defense flight test, resulting in the intercept of two medium-range ballistic missile targets. The flight test was planned more than a year ago, and is not in any way connected to events in the Middle East.

The test was conducted in the vicinity of the U.S. Army Kwajalein Atoll/Reagan Test Site and surrounding areas in the western Pacific. The test stressed the ability of the Aegis Ballistic Missile Defense (BMD) and Terminal High Altitude Area Defense (THAAD) weapon systems to function in a layered defense architecture and defeat a raid of two near-simultaneous ballistic missile targets.

The two medium-range ballistic missile targets were launched on operationally realistic trajectories towards a defended area near Kwajalein. Along with overhead space assets providing launch alerts, an Army-Navy/Transportable Radar Surveillance and Control (AN/TPY-2) radar in Forward Based Mode detected the targets and relayed track information to the Command, Control, Battle Management, and Communications (C2BMC) system for further transmission to defending BMDS assets.

The USS Decatur with its Aegis Weapon System detected and tracked the first target with its onboard AN/SPY-1 radar. The Aegis BMD weapon system developed a fire control solution, launched a Standard Missile-3 (SM-3) Block IA missile, and successfully intercepted the target.

In a demonstration of BMDS layered defense capabilities, a second AN/TPY-2 radar in Terminal Mode, located with the THAAD weapon system, acquired and tracked the target missiles. THAAD developed a fire control solution, launched a THAAD interceptor missile, and successfully intercepted the second medium-range ballistic missile target. THAAD was operated by soldiers from the Alpha Battery, 2nd Air Defense Artillery Regiment. As a planned demonstration of THAAD's layered defense capabilities, a second THAAD interceptor was launched at the target destroyed by Aegis as a contingency in the event the SM-3 did not achieve an intercept.

Initial indications are that all components performed as designed. MDA officials will extensively assess and evaluate system performance based upon telemetry and other data obtained during the test.

The event, a designated Flight Test Operational-01 (FTO-01), demonstrated integrated, layered, regional missile defense capabilities to defeat a raid of two threat-representative medium-range ballistic missiles in a combined live-fire operational test. Soldiers, sailors, and airmen from multiple combatant commands operated the systems, and were provided a unique opportunity to refine operational doctrine and tactics while increasing confidence in the execution of integrated air and missile defense plans.[76]

September 18, 2013, Test. MDA states that in this flight test,

The Missile Defense Agency (MDA), U.S. Pacific Command, and U.S. Navy sailors aboard the USS Lake Erie (CG 70) successfully conducted a flight test today of the Aegis Ballistic Missile Defense (BMD) system, resulting in the intercept of a complex separating short-

---

[76] Missile Defense Agency press release 13-News-0007, dated September 10, 2013, entitled "Successful Missile Defense Test Against Multiple Targets." See also Megan Eckstein, "Aegis BMDS, THAAD Successful In Complex MDA Flight Test," *Defense Daily*, September 11, 2013: 1; and Amy Butler, "MDA Goes Two For Two In Operational Test," *Aerospace Daily & Defense Report*, September 11, 2013: 4.

range ballistic missile target over the Pacific Ocean by the Aegis BMD 4.0 Weapon System and a Standard Missile-3 (SM-3) Block IB guided missile.

At approximately 2:30 p m. Hawaii Standard Time (8:30 p m. EDT), a complex separating short-range ballistic missile target was launched from the Pacific Missile Range Facility on Kauai, Hawaii. The target flew northwest towards a broad ocean area of the Pacific Ocean. Following target launch, the USS Lake Erie detected and tracked the missile with its onboard AN/SPY-1 radar. The ship, equipped with the second-generation Aegis BMD weapon system, developed a fire control solution and launched two SM-3 Block IB guided missiles to engage the target. The first SM-3 that was launched successfully intercepted the target warhead. This was the first salvo mission of two SM-3 Block IB guided missiles launched against a single separating target.

Program officials will assess and evaluate system performance based upon telemetry and other data obtained during the test.

This test exercised the latest version of the second-generation Aegis BMD Weapon System, capable of engaging longer range and more sophisticated ballistic missiles. This was an operationally realistic test, in which the target's launch time and bearing are not known in advance, and the target complex was the most difficult target engaged to date.[77]

October 3, 2013, Test. MDA states that in this flight test,

> The Missile Defense Agency (MDA), U.S. Pacific Command, and U.S. Navy sailors aboard the USS Lake Erie (CG 70) successfully conducted an operational flight test of the Aegis Ballistic Missile Defense (BMD) system, resulting in the intercept of a medium-range ballistic missile target over the Pacific Ocean by the Aegis BMD 4.0 Weapon System and a Standard Missile-3 (SM-3) Block IB guided missile.
>
> At approximately 7:33 p m. Hawaii Standard Time, Oct. 3 (1:33 a m. EDT, Oct.4), a medium-range ballistic missile target was launched from the Pacific Missile Range Facility on Kauai, Hawaii. The target flew northwest towards a broad ocean area of the Pacific Ocean. Following target launch, the USS Lake Erie detected and tracked the missile with its onboard AN/SPY-1 radar. The ship, equipped with the second-generation Aegis BMD weapon system, developed a fire control solution and launched the SM-3 Block IB guided missile to engage the target. The SM-3 maneuvered to a point in space and released its kinetic warhead. The kinetic warhead acquired the target reentry vehicle, diverted into its path, and, using only the force of a direct impact, engaged and destroyed the target.
>
> Program officials will assess and evaluate system performance based upon telemetry and other data obtained during the test.
>
> This test exercised the latest version of the second-generation Aegis BMD Weapon System, capable of engaging longer range and more sophisticated ballistic missiles.[78]

---

[77] Missile Defense Agency press release 13-News-0008, dated September 18, 2013, entitled "Aegis Ballistic Missile Defense System Completes Successful Intercept Flight Test." See also Mike McCarthy, "Pentagon Succeeds At Sea-Based Missile Defense Test," *Defense Daily*, September 20, 2013: 1; Amy Butler, "Aegis Intercepts In First-Ever Salvo Test," *Aerospace Daily & Defense Report*, September 20, 2013: 3; and Jason Sherman and John Liang, "Missile Defense Agency's SM-3 Block IB Intercepts Target In Salvo Fire," *Inside the Navy*, September 23, 2013.

[78] Missile Defense Agency press release 13-News-0009, dated October 4, 2013, entitled "Aegis Ballistic Missile Defense System Completes Successful Intercept Flight Test." See also Michael Fabey, "Aegis Completes Another Intercept Test," *Aerospace Daily & Defense Report*, October 7, 2013: 2; Jason Sherman, "SM-3 Block IB Completes (continued...)

Endo-Atmospheric (SM-2 Block IV) Flight Tests

The Aegis BMD system using the SM-2 Block IV interceptor has achieved three successful endo-atmospheric intercepts in three at-sea attempts, the first occurring on May 24, 2006,[79] the second on June 5, 2008,[80] and the third on March 26, 2009.[81]

(...continued)

IOT&E With A Bang, Full-Rate Production Review," *Inside the Navy*, October 7, 2013; Mike McCarthy, "Aegis Missile Defense Test Scores Hit," *Defense Daily*, October 7, 2013: 4.

[79] See Missile Defense Agency, "First at-Sea Demonstration of Sea-Based Terminal Capability Successfully Completed," May 24, 2006 (06-FYI-0079); Gregg K. Kakesako, "Missile Defense System Makes History," *Honolulu Star-Bulletin*, May 25, 2006; Audrey McAvoy, "Ship Shoots Down Test Missile For The First Time," *NavyTimes.com*, May 25, 2006; "Navy, MDA Announce First Terminal Sea-Based Intercept," *Aerospace Daily & Defense Report*, May 26, 2006; Zachary M. Peterson, "Navy Conducts First Sea-Based Terminal Phase Missile Defense Test," *Inside the Navy*, May 29, 2006; and Jeremy Singer, "Sea-Based Terminal May Boost U.S. Missile Defense Capability," *Space News* (*www.space.com*), June 12, 2006.

[80] See Missile Defense Agency, "Successful Sea-Based Missile Defense Intercept," June 5, 2008 (08-NEWS-0068); Dave Ahearn, "Aegis, SM-2 Interceptors Kill Target Missile In Terminal-Phase Success," *Defense Daily,* June 6, 2008.

[81] "Navy Completes Air and Ballistic Missile Exercise," *Navy News Service*, March 26, 2009.

Appendix B. Homeporting of U.S. Navy Aegis BMD Ships at Rota, Spain

This appendix presents additional background information on the Navy's plan to homeport four BMD-capable Aegis destroyers at Rota, Spain.

As part of the October 5, 2011, U.S.-Spain joint announcement of the plan, the Prime Minister of Spain, Jose Luis Rodriguez Zapatero, stated in part:

> This meeting marks a step forward on the path that we set for ourselves less than a year ago at the Lisbon Summit, aiming to make NATO an Alliance that is "more effective, engaged and efficient than ever before", in the words of [NATO] Secretary-General Rasmussen.
>
> At that historic Summit, decisions of enormous importance for the future of the Alliance were taken, such as the New Strategic Concept to face the new challenges of the 21st century, and the establishment of a new command structure that is leaner and more flexible, and improved.
>
> Besides these two important innovations, and as a consequence of them, the allies decided to develop an Anti-Missile Defence System....
>
> As you will recall, as a consequence of this new structure launched in Lisbon, Spain obtained an installation of great importance within NATO's Command and Control Structure: the Combined Air Operations Centre (CAOC) in Torrejón de Ardoz, Spain.
>
> This Centre, together with the Centre in Uedem, Germany, will form part of the air command and control system which is to include the anti-missile defence that the Alliance is going to implement.
>
> Together with this land-based component of the new air defence system, I can inform you that Spain is also going to support, starting in 2013, an important part of the system's naval element.
>
> In recent months, the different options have been studied, and finally, it was decided that Spain should be the site for this component of the system, due to its geostrategic location and its position as gateway to the Mediterranean.
>
> Specifically, the United States is going to deploy, as its contribution to NATO's Anti-Missile Defence System, a total of four vessels equipped with the AEGIS system, to be based in Rota.
>
> This means that Rota is going to become a support centre for vessel deployment, enabling them to join multinational forces or carry out NATO missions in international waters, particularly in the Mediterranean....
>
> Moreover, this initiative will have a positive impact, in socio-economic terms, on our country, and most especially on the Bay of Cadiz.
>
> Permanently basing four vessels in Rota will require investing in the Base's infrastructure, and contracts with service providers, thus generating approximately a thousand new jobs, both directly and indirectly.

For the shipyards, and for Spain's defence industry, the foreseeable impact will also be highly positive, as the USA is considering conducting the vessels' maintenance and upkeep at the nearby San Fernando shipyards, in the province of Cadiz. In addition, there will be significant transfer of state-of-the-art technology, from which Spain can benefit.[82]

As part of the same joint announcement, Secretary of Defense Leon Panetta stated in part:

With four Aegis ships at Rota, the alliance is significantly boosting combined naval capabilities in the Mediterranean, and enhancing our ability to ensure the security of this vital region. This relocation of assets takes place as part of the United States' ongoing effort to better position forces and defensive capabilities in coordination with our European allies and partners.

This announcement should send a very strong signal that the United States is continuing to invest in this alliance, and that we are committed to our defense relationship with Europe even as we face growing budget constraints at home....

Alongside important agreements that were recently concluded with Romania, Poland, and Turkey, Spain's decision represents a critical step in implementing the European Phased Adaptive Approach, as our leaders agreed to in Lisbon....

Beyond missile defense, the Aegis destroyers will perform a variety of other important missions, including participating in the Standing NATO Maritime Groups, as well as joining in naval exercises, port visits, and maritime security cooperation activities....

The agreement also enables the United States to provide rapid and responsive support to the U.S. Africa and U.S. Central Commands, as needed.[83]

An October 5, 2011, press report stated:

A senior U.S. defense official said making the [ships'] base at Rota, on Spain's southwestern Atlantic coast near Cadiz, would reduce the numbers of [BMD-capable Aegis] ships needed for the [EPAA] system.

"You [would] probably need 10 of these ships if they were based in the eastern U.S. to be able to ... transit across the ocean back and forth to [keep the same number on] patrol in the Med," he said.

The U.S. official said the United States was committed to having at least one ship on station at all times in the eastern Mediterranean, where their anti-missile missiles would be most effective. Having them based in Rota would enable more than one to be in the eastern Mediterranean as needed.

---

[82] "Announcement on missile defence cooperation by NATO Secretary General Anders Fogh Rasmussen, the Prime Minister of Spain, Jose Luis Rodriguez Zapatero and US Defense Secretary Leon Panetta," October 5, 2011, accessed October 6, 2011, at http://www.nato.int/cps/en/SID-107ADE55-FF83A6B8/natolive/opinions_78838 htm.

[83] "Announcement on missile defence cooperation by NATO Secretary General Anders Fogh Rasmussen, the Prime Minister of Spain, Jose Luis Rodriguez Zapatero and US Defense Secretary Leon Panetta," October 5, 2011, accessed October 6, 2011, at http://www.nato.int/cps/en/SID-107ADE55-FF83A6B8/natolive/opinions_78838 htm. See also "SECDEF Announces Stationing of Aegis Ships at Rota, Spain," accessed October 6, 2011, at http://www navy.mil/search/display.asp?story_id=63109.

The ships also would be part of the pool of vessels available to participate in standing NATO maritime groups, which are used to counter piracy and for other missions, he said.[84]

An October 10, 2011, press report stated:

> "Our plan is to have the first couple [of ships] there in 2014 and the next two in about 2015," said Cmdr. Marc Boyd, spokesman for [U.S. Navy] 6th Fleet. Boyd added: "It's really early in the process and we haven't selected any of the ships yet." Boyd said the shift will bring an estimated 1,300 sailors and Navy civilians and 2,100 dependents to Naval Station Rota, which would double the base's ranks. Naval Station Rota spokesman Lt. j.g. Jason Fischer said the base now has 1,067 sailors....
>
> The three piers at the base primarily support Navy ships passing through on port calls.
>
> Boyd said 6th Fleet is considering plans to add base infrastructure and maintenance facilities to support the ships, as well as additional housing for crews, "but the base is pretty suited as it is now."[85]

---

[84] David Brunnstrom and David Alexander, "Spain To Host U.S. Missile Defense Ships," *Reuters*, October 5, 2011. Ellipsis as in original.

[85] Sam Fellman, "U.S. To Base Anti-Missile Ships in Spain," *Defense News*, October 10, 2011: 76.

Appendix C. Allied Participation and Interest in Aegis BMD Program

This appendix presents additional background information on allied participation and interest in the Aegis BMD program.

Japan

A November 5, 2013, press report states:

> The Defense Ministry [of Japan] plans to order two more Aegis destroyers capable of intercepting ballistic missiles in view of the continuing nuclear and missile threats from North Korea, government sources said Tuesday [November 5].
>
> The ministry will soon start negotiations with the Finance Ministry on the plan to bring the number of Aegis destroyers operated by the Maritime Self-Defense Force to eight.
>
> The Defense Ministry intends to include the plan in new defense guidelines that spell out Japan's security policies for the coming decade. The government will draw up the guidelines by the end of the year.
>
> The ministry plans to put the two new vessels into commission during the decade covered by the new guidelines.
>
> Four of the MSDF's six Aegis destroyers are currently equipped with the missile defense system that can shoot down ballistic missiles in space. The other two are being fitted with the system.
>
> At least two are needed to cover the entire Japanese archipelago with the ballistic missile defense system, though more provide better protection. However, at least one is always in port for required maintenance.[86]

Other Countries

A September 16, 2013, press report states:

> One of the UK Royal Navy's new Type 45 destroyers is conducting tests to establish whether the warships could provide British forces with theater ballistic-missile defense (TBMD) capabilities for the first time, according to the head of the Royal Navy.
>
> First Sea Lord Adm. Sir George Zambellas said during a speech to industry executives and military personnel on the opening day of the DSEi defense exhibition that the "type is on trials in the Pacific to explore the ballistic-missile defense capabilities that are ready to be exploited, bringing strategic opportunities to the vessel."

---

[86] "Japan To Build Two More Aegis Destroyers To Boost Missile Defense," *The Japan Times* (*www.japantimes.co.jp*), November 5, 2013. See also "Govt To Build 2 More Aegis Ships," *Yomiuri Shimbun* (http://the-japan-news.com), November 6, 2013.

The Type 45 destroyer Daring, one of six Type 45s built by BAE Systems for the Royal Navy, has been in the Pacific for several weeks, having departed its Portsmouth base this summer for a wide-ranging nine-month deploy-ment, which the Royal Navy said in May would include science and technology trials. The work is being done as part of a US Missile Defense Agency (MDA) research and development test....

In May, the UK Defence Ministry confirmed it was talking to Aster 30 partners France and Italy about developing an extended-range version of a missile already used by the French and Italian armies to intercept incoming missiles While there is no program to adapt the Type 45 to include TBMD capability, the trials support the possibility of such a move once a decision whether to go down that route is made by the British government.[87]

A March 18, 2013, press report states:

Raytheon has discussed a possible pooling arrangement with three navies in northern Europe to make its SM-3 ballistic missile inter-ceptor more affordable, according to a senior company executive.

Speaking after a successful test of a new data link enabling the SM-3 to communicate with X-band radars operated by Dutch, Danish and Ger-man warships, George Mavko, director of European missile defense at Raytheon Missile Systems, said the idea of a pooling arrangement had been raised by the company, even though none of the countries are pursuing procurement at this point....

While all three European navies have expressed an interest in the capability of the SM-3 to engage ballistic missiles at ranges outside the atmosphere, none appear close to actually procuring the missiles....

Instead, led by the Dutch, the initial moves appear focused on updating naval X-band radars and other systems so they can provide target data to SM-3 missiles even if they can't prosecute their own attack....

Aside from the pooling idea, Raytheon also recently opened discussions with the U.S. Missile Defense Agency over co-production of SM-3 systems in Europe to sweeten any future deal, Mavko said....

Small bits of the missile are already produced in Europe, although it was "too early to imply the U.S. is willing to release any major subsystems to other countries for co-production," Mavko said....

Raytheon has been cooperating with the Dutch Navy for several years, exploring the potential of the SM-3 to talk to X-band radars. The Dutch have co-funded a study with the U.S. government on the feasibil-ity of a dual-band data link; the study is due to be extended into a second phase. The German government has agreed to participate this time.[88]

A March 11, 2013, press report states:

The Eurosam SAMP/T surface-to-air missile system has destroyed a representative theater ballistic missile during a test in France.

---

[87] Andrew Chuter, "UK Royal Navy Examines BMD Capabilities," *Defense News*, September 16, 2013: 38.

[88] Andrew Chuter, "Raytheon Pushes European SM-3 Missile Pool," *Defense News*, March 18, 2013: 4.

The March 6 test saw a joint Italian and French team engage an aircraft-launched target using an Aster 30 missile fired from the Biscarosse missile test center on the Bay of Biscay coast.

According to French government defense procurement agency the DGA, the operational evaluation firing was jointly carried out by the Italian 4th Artillery Regiment of Mantova with the French military airborne test center (CEAM) of Mont-de-Marsan. In a change from previous interceptions, the SAMP/T used Link 16 data links to provide target information. The test also was the first to use what Eurosam calls a NATO environment in terms of command and control of the weapon, rather than simply using French sensors.

The company says the firing was as "close to what would be an operational use for an anti-theater ballistic missile mission under the aegis of the alliance Active Layered Theater Ballistic Missile Defense program."

The company adds, "The NATO Ballistic Missile Defense Operations Cell, located in Ramstein, Germany, was in the loop via Link 16 network."[89]

Another March 11, 2013, press report states:

Joint US and European testing of command, control, communications and radar systems are underway to demonstrate the feasibility of integration of European radars and command and control systems into a future missile defense systems based on the planned European Phased Adaptive Approach (EPAA) utilizing the several AEGIS destroyers or cruisers to be based in Spain, land-based SM-3 interceptors to be stationed in Romania and Poland, along with SPY-2 radars sites. These assets are to be complemented by a number of European deployed radar sites.

In recent weeks tests were carried out to evaluate such integration. Last week Raytheon reported about a recent trial that showed that a radar used by Dutch, German and Danish navies could provide target information to the interceptor. The current radar installed on the Dutch frigates is incompatible with the AEGIS/SM-3 link operating over S-band. The demonstration which took place at the Den Helder military test range validated a datalink that allows the missile to receive information from the Thales sensor while retaining the ability to communicate with Aegis combat ships used by the U.S. Navy. Generally, The Dutch, German and Danish navies datalinks are operating on X bands, while Norway, Spain and the U.S. operate AEGIS frigates communicating with their interceptors over the S band. To avoid unique configurations of missiles, Raytheon has developed a dual-band datalink which enables the same missile to communicate in both bands. This dual-band datalink was first tested in 2011.[90]

A March 8, 2013, press report states:

The British Royal Navy is exploring the possibility of outfitting its newest class of destroyers with a ballistic missile defense capability.

The Defence Ministry said this week it wants to examine the potential for the Type 45 destroyers to play a role in defending the United Kingdom and allies from the threat of

---

[89] Tony Osborne, "European SAMP/T Destroys Ballistic Missile In Test," *Aerospace Daily & Defense Report*, March 11, 2013: 3.

[90] Tamir Eshel, "Integrating European Radars with AEGIS/SM-3 Missile Defenses," *Defense Update* (http://defense-update.com), March 11, 2013, accessed March 20, 2013 at http://defense-update.com/20130311_integrating-european-radars-with-aegissm-3-missile-defenses.html.

ballistic missiles. The ministry said it will build on its relationship with the Pentagon's Missile Defense Agency to look at the option....

The joint Defence Ministry and industry-run U.K. Missile Defence Center (MDC) plans to take part in a trial that for the first time will use a Type 45 in a research and development program with their American counterparts.

That will involve testing the Sampson radar, which is part of the Sea Viper missile system, in detecting and tracking ballistic missiles, the ministry said.

The is no program to deploy ballistic missile defense on Type 45s but the MDC has in recent years been exploring the option for the destroyers.

"It will be a step change to be able to work so closely with such a ship in an emerging area of defense," MDC head Simon Pavitt said in a statement. "Working with an operational platform will make a significant difference to our level of understanding and could contribute both financially and technically towards any future program."[91]

An October 2012 article stated:

The Royal Netherlands Navy's (RNLN's) four De Zeven Provincien-class LCF air defence and command frigates are to receive a substantially upgraded and rearchitectured SMART-L D-band volume search radar that will give the ships a ballistic missile defence (BMD) early warning capability.

Thales Nederland received a EUR116 million (USD145 million) contract from the Netherlands' Defence Materiel Organisation (DMO) in June 2012 for the new extended-range sensor known as 'SMART-L EWC'. This new variant of SMART-L, which builds oni the results of a previous Extended Long Range (ELR) capability demonstration, will push instrumented range out to 2,000 km; improve elevation coverage; introduce new wave forms and processing optimised for the detection and tracking of very-high-velocity ballistic missile targets at altitude; and enable estimation of trajectories, launch sites and points of impact. At the same time, all SMART-L volume air search functionality will be retained.[92]

A journal article published in the summer of 2012 states:

Today the steady growth of Aegis-capable ships in the U.S. Navy—as well as an increasing number of world navies fielding such ships—presents new opportunities and challenges....

... the Aegis BMD capabilities present in the navies of U.S. allies and friends can now provide the Global Maritime Partnership with a means to address the "high end" of the kill chain with combined, coordinated, ballistic-missile defense: the Aegis BMD Global Enterprise.

This potential is already manifest in the Asia-Pacific region in the close working relationship between the United States and Japan. Korea and Australia could well join this Aegis network

---

[91] Mike McCarthy, "U.K. Examining Sea-Based Missile Defense," *Defense Daily*, March 8, 2013: 10. See also "British Destroyer to Participate in U.S. Missile Defense Trials," *Defense Update* (http://defense-update.com), March 7, 2013, accessed March 27, 2013, at http://defense-update.com/20130307_british-destroyer-to-participate-in-u-s-missile-defense-trials.html.

[92] Kate Tringham, "Warning Signs: Netherlands Evolves SMART-L Radar For Ballistic Missile Defence Mission," *Jane's International Defence Review*, October 2012: 28-29.

soon, giving the four governments the means to address not only territorial BMD but also coordinated BMD of fleet units operating together. In Europe, plans are well along to provide robust territorial defense of European nations with ALTBMD [active layered theater BMD] and the EPAA. Together, these systems provide a nascent BMD capability today and promise an even more robust capability as the EPAA evolves over the next decade and a half.

But as demonstrated in Iraq, Afghanistan, and now Libya, NATO and the nations of Europe have equities often well beyond the territorial boundaries of the European continent. Also, a European military deployed beyond Europe's borders will always have a naval component. This is therefore a propitious time to begin to link European allies more completely into an Aegis BMD Global Enterprise in much the same way the U.S. Navy is linked to its Asia-Pacific partners—Japan today, Korea soon, and thereafter Australia in the near future—in a high-end Aegis BMD Global Maritime Partnership....

The diffusion of Aegis BMD capability abroad is occurring quietly. Governments that have made naval force-structure investment decisions based primarily on inwardly focused national interests have discovered that their investments also enable them to combine their resources in collective defense....

This effort to create a broad BMD enterprise builds on the current participation of allied navies in the Aegis program. This global effort started with a foreign military sales relationship with Japan, subsequently expanded to relationships with Australia and Korea, and now includes a commercial connection with Spain as well as an enterprise between Norway and Spain.22 Several other states have expressed interest in acquiring the Aegis weapon system and Aegis BMD. Importantly, Australia and other countries that are acquiring the Aegis system are stipulating that the systems they buy must have the capability of adding BMD in the future....

In Europe, the decision as to whether and how to connect the European NATO allies' short- and medium-range theater missile-defense systems to the U.S. long-range missile defense system will be critical to the coherence of alliance-wide BMD. A high level of commitment to international partnership on the parts of both the United States and its allies—already evinced by ALTBMD and C2BMC shared situational-awareness tests—will encourage interoperability initiatives. This interoperability will, in turn, help ensure the success of the U.S. Phased Adaptive Approach....

Close cooperation in the area of Aegis BMD between the United States and Japan, possibly Korea, and potentially Australia does not in itself qualify as an "Aegis BMD Global Enterprise." But to include European nations in an Aegis-afloat enterprise of capabilities approaching those planned for the ALTBMD/EPAA system would....

European navies are now deployed worldwide fulfilling the vision of a Global Maritime Partnership: supporting operations in Iraq and Afghanistan, fighting in Libya, conducting antipiracy patrols in the Horn of Africa and elsewhere, and supporting humanitarian assistance operations around the world. There could be no more propitious time to begin to link more completely European allies in an Aegis BMD Global Enterprise, in much the same way the U.S. Navy is now linked to its Asia-Pacific partners in a high-end Aegis BMD Global Maritime Partnership....

But it is unlikely that such a venture would succeed without ongoing U.S. leadership, the same sort of leadership that is supporting sea-based Aegis BMD for territorial and fleet ballistic-missile defense today in the northeast Pacific as well as sea-based and land-based ballistic territorial missile defense in Europe. Clearly, U.S. leadership could be what accelerates the morphing of a now-nascent Aegis BMD Global Enterprise in Europe into a global Aegis BMD afloat capability....

There is a growing worldwide commitment to Aegis ballistic-missile defense, a commitment with broad potential to field an international global enterprise capable of defending against the most imminent, and growing, threat to nations and navies, on land and at sea alike—the threat of ballistic missiles, particularly those armed with weapons of mass destruction.[93]

A May 7, 2012, press report states:

The German Navy's fleet of frigates could be upgraded to deploy Raytheon's [RTN] Standard Missile-3 to participate in NATO's ballistic missile defense program if the modifications were approved by the government, Germany's top naval officer recently said.

Vice Admiral Axel Schimpf, the counterpart to the U.S. Navy's chief of naval operations, said in a recently published article that the F124 frigates are capable of being upgraded to play a vital role in ballistic missile defense (BMD).

"The German Navy, with the F124 Frigates in their current configuration, has a weapon system at their disposal which forms the basis for capability enhancements for (German) armed forces' participation in various roles," according to a translation of an article he penned in Marine Forum, a publication of the German Maritime Institute.

One option, Schimpf said, would be to upgrade the F124s' SMART-L and Active Phased Array Radar (APAR) combat management system, along with the Mk-41 vertical launch system to accommodate the SM-3....

The enhancements would be one way for Germany to participate in the Obama administration's European Phased Adaptive Approach (EPAA) embraced by NATO, and could be done in cooperation with Denmark or the Netherlands, Schimpf said....

The German government has not made on decisions on whether to adapt its frigates for ballistic missile defense, and Germany's role in EPAA is the source of ongoing political discussions in Berlin ahead of NATO's May 20-21 summit in Chicago....

Only a handful of NATO allies deploy the Aegis combat system on ships, and Germany is not one of them. Germany's combat system does not operate on an S-band frequency used on Aegis. Raytheon, however, says it has developed a duel band data link that would allow the combat system on allied ships to talk to the SM-3 and guide it to targets.[94]

An October 3, 2011, press report stated that

The Netherlands, which has had a longtime interest in a missile shield, is pressing ahead to build up its own capabilities. The Dutch defense ministry plans to expand the capabilities of the Thales Smart-L radar on Dutch frigates to take on BMD roles. The program's value is estimated at €100-250 million, including logistics support and spares.

Other European navies using the sensor may follow the Dutch lead.

---

[93] Brad Hicks, George Galdorisi, and Scott C. Truver, "The Aegis BMD Global Enterprise," *Naval War College Review*, Summer 2012: 65-80.

[94] Mike McCarthy, "Raytheon's SM-3 An Option For German Role In Missile Defense, Admiral Says," *Defense Daily*, May 7, 2012: 9.

Dutch Defense Minister Hans Hillen notes that the Smart-L effort would help address the BMD sensor shortage within the NATO alliance. Citing NATO's decision last year to take a more expansive approach to BMD, Hillen says Smart-L could give the ALTBMD [Active Layered Theater BMD] command-and control backbone the required long-range target-detection analysis to help identify where a threat originates.

The Netherlands has already carried out a sensor trial for the expanded role in cooperation with the U.S. Navy. The move does not include the purchase of Raytheon Standard Missile SM-3 interceptors.

Both hardware and software modifications to the combat management system are needed. All four [of the Dutch navy's] De Zeven Provincien-class frigates would be modified to ensure that two can be deployed, even as one is in maintenance and the fourth is being readied for operations.

Thales is due to complete a series of studies to prepare for the acquisition of the upgrade in the third quarter of 2012. The goal is to have the first frigates ready for operations by 2017. All four should be upgraded by the end of that year.

Although the Netherlands is leading the program, other Smart-L users, including the German navy and Denmark, have been monitoring the effort. France also has shown interest in the system, Hillen said in a letter to legislators.

France also wants to upgrade its Aster 30 interceptor to give it a basic BMD capability, although a formal contract has not been awarded....

Raytheon, meanwhile, is still fighting to win a foothold for its Standard Missile 3 (SM-3) in Europe. The company continues its push to persuade continental navies to embrace the SM-3 Block 1B for missile defense roles, and says it has largely validated the dual-mode data link that would be key to the concept.

The data link would feature both S- and X-band capability—the former to support the Aegis radar system used by the U.S. and others, and the latter for the Smart-L/APAR (active phased array radar) combination used, for instance, by the Dutch navy.[95]

A September 2011 press report states:

The gulf in sea-based ballistic missile defence (BMD) capability between the navies of NATO's European member states and the US Navy (USN) was brought into stark relief by the recent deployment of the Ticonderoga-class cruiser USS Monterey to the Mediterranean and Black Sea region, as the first element of the United States' European Phased Adaptive Approach (EPAA) for missile defence....

However, this situation is about to change as European NATO nations are committing their naval assets to BMD in response to evolving alliance policy towards developing a BMD architecture to protect the continent from perceived threats emanating from the Middle East.

---

[95] Robert Wall, Amy Svitak, and Amy Butler, "Supporting Role," *Aviation Week & Space Technology*, October 3, 2011: 28-29. A shorter version of the story was published as Robert Wall, "Dutch Press Forward On Ship-Based Missile Defense Effort," *Aerospace Daily & Defense Report*, September 27, 2011: 4. See also Menno Steketee, "Dutch Frigates to Gain BMD Capability," *Jane's Navy International* (*Janes.com*), September 28, 2011. (The print version of the report appeared under the same article title in the November 2011 issue of *Jane's Navy International*, page 8.

NATO embarked on an Active Layered Theatre Ballistic Missile Defence System (ALTBMDS) programme in September 2005, following a two-year feasibility study. Its initial focus was the protection of deployed alliance forces and high-value assets against short- and medium-range threats. At the November 2010 Lisbon Summit, political leaders from NATO states committed to expanding that remit to include the defence of the alliance's European territory.

ALTBMD is providing a C2 framework on which to build a scalable and adaptable BMD 'system of systems' architecture, integrating new national systems as they are committed to the alliance and enabling a complete lower- and upper-layer capability covering Europe to be fielded. The first of these, Capability 1, with initial operational capability planned for the 2012 timeframe, integrates C2 infrastructure, sensors and ground-based Patriot interceptors. The expansion to provide upper-layer defence is due to achieve full operational capability between 2015 and 2016.

The US contribution to this architecture is the EPAA set out by the Obama administration in September 2009....

There is evidence that the EPAA has acted as a spur for some European nations to make a more coherent contribution to the NATO BMD construct, particularly in the maritime domain, as they seek to maintain sovereignty in the development and integration of indigenous BMD systems and defence of their territories.

A number of classes of the latest generation of anti-air warfare (AAW) combatants with the potential to acquire a BMD capability are either operational or entering service in the navies of Denmark, France, Germany, Italy, the Netherlands, Norway, Spain and the UK. These offer the attributes of flexibility in deployment, mobility and sustainability inherent in naval platforms and could operate as effective sensor nodes even without an organic intercept capability.

They would be able to forward deploy close to the origin of the threat and act as force multipliers in this role by providing early warning of launches and cueing of off-board interceptor systems with the provision of timely and accurate impact point prediction and missile tracks, together with launch point prediction for counter-targeting.[96]

---

[96] Charles Hollosi, "European Fleets Respond to Ballistic Missile Threats," *Jane's Navy International*, September 2011: 23-24, 26-30.

Author Contact Information

Ronald O'Rourke
Specialist in Naval Affairs
rorourke@crs.loc.gov, 7-7610

www.ingramcontent.com/pod-product-compliance
Lightning Source LLC
Chambersburg PA
CBHW05201128052б
45793CB00005B/929